# Grimm Fairy Tales™ Myths & Legends

zenescope

LIBRARY DISCARD
MOOSE JAW PUBLIC LIBRARY
NON-RETURNABLE

# Grimm Fairy Tales Myths & Legends

Grimm Fairy Tales Created by
Joe Brusha
Ralph Tedesco

Story by
Raven Gregory
Joe Brusha
Ralph Tedesco
Troy Brownfield

Written by
Raven Gregory
Troy Brownfield

Trade Design by
Christopher Cote

Trade Edited by
Ralph Tedesco
Hannah Gorfinkel
Matt Rogers

This volume reprints the comic series Grimm Fairy Tales Myths & Legends issues #16, 17, and 22-25 published by Zenescope Entertainment.

www.zenescope.com

First Edition, March 2013
ISBN: 978-1-937068-83-7

WWW.ZENESCOPE.COM
FACEBOOK.COM/ZENESCOPE

ZENESCOPE ENTERTAINMENT, INC.
**Joe Brusha** • President & Chief Creative Officer
**Ralph Tedesco** • Editor-in-Chief
**Jennifer Bermel** • Director of Licensing & Business Development
**Raven Gregory** • Executive Editor
**Anthony Spay** • Art Director
**Christopher Cote** • Production Manager
**Dave Franchini** • Direct Market Sales & Customer Service
**Stephen Haberman** • Marketing Manager

Grimm Fairy Tales Myths & Legends Trade Paperback Vol. 5, March, 2013. First Printing. Published by Zenescope Entertainment Inc., 433 Caredean Drive, Ste. C, Horsham, Pennsylvania 19044. Zenescope and its logos are ® and © 2013 Zenescope Entertainment Inc. all rights reserved. Grimm Fairy Tales Myths & Legends, its logo and all characters and their likeness are © and ™ 2013 Zenescope Entertainment. Any similarities to persons (living or dead), events, institutions, or locales are purely coincidental. No portion of this publication may be reproduced or transmitted, in any form or by any means, without the express written permission of Zenescope Entertainment Inc. except for artwork used for review purposes. Printed in Canada.

# Grimm Fairy Tales™ Myths & Legends

# Chapter One: The Gathering, Part 1

Story by Raven Gregory, Joe Brusha, and Ralph Tedesco

Written by Raven Gregory • Art by Joyce Mauriera and Ilias Kyriazis

Colors by Jeff Balke, Sean Forney, and Ramon Ignacio Bunge

"LOT OF SECURITY FOR A STATUE, DON'T YOU THINK?"
"LONG AS THEY'RE WILLING TO FORK OUT THE OVERTIME ON THIS I COULD REALLY CARE LESS."
"JUST FOUND OUT MY KID HAS TO GET BRACES. YOU KNOW HOW MUCH THAT SHIT COSTS?"
NOT A CLUE. THAT'S WHY I DON'T HAVE KIDS. SHIT'S EXPENSIVE.
YOU DON'T HAVE A KID BECAUSE NO WOMAN IN HER RIGHT MIND WOULD HAVE SEX WITH YOU.
WHAT'S THAT SUPPOSED TO MEAN?
IT MEANS THAT EVERY TIME WE GO OUT AND TRY AND TALK TO GIRLS YOU SCARE THEM ALL AWAY BECAUSE EVERYONE THINKS YOU'RE A SERIAL KILLER.
WHATEVER. I GET GIRLS.
BITE ME.
YOU GUYS WANT TO HIT THE BAR AFTER THIS?
SURE, NOT LIKE I HAVE ANYTHING--

KATHOOM

HELP.
MY FOOT'S CAUGHT.
I THINK MY ARM'S BROKEN.
UNNGH.
Oh, GOD.
SOMEONE. ANYONE.
WE NEED HELP.
TUD

Ah, THERE YOU ARE.

I HAVE BEEN LOOKING FOR *YOU* FOR SOME TIME.
CRASH
WHY, *HELLO* THERE.

"SOMEONE IS GOING TO BE **QUITE** UPSET ABOUT LOSING YOU."
COME.
KNOCK KNOCK

HAS IT ARRIVED YET, MORRIGAN?
THERE HAS BEEN A ***PROBLEM.***
WHAT PROBLEM?
THE TRANSPORT WAS ***ATTACKED.*** THE ***SHARD*** WAS ***TAKEN.***
BY WHOM?

BABA YAGA.

...
***FIND*** HER. ***FIND*** THE SHARD.
***NOW!***

HEY! YOU CAN'T GO IN THERE, DETECTIVE. CHIEF CALLED IT IN.
WHAT'D THEY TAKE?
NO IDEA WHAT THEY HAD IN THERE, BUT WHATEVER IT WAS HAS A LOT OF POWERFUL PEOPLE STICKING THEIR NOSES IN PLACES WHERE--
WHERE WHAT?
WHAT THE HELL IS THIS?
WHY ISN'T ANYONE MOVING?
IT HAS BEGUN, JUST AS WE FEARED.

ANY IDEA WHAT HAPPENED HERE?
WE THINK THE TRUCK WAS THE *TARGET.* NO IDEA WHAT KIND OF ARTILLERY THEY USED. PLACE LOOKS LIKE A GODDAMN *WAR* ZONE.
HEY? BUDDY? YOU OKAY?
*HELLO?*
PONG

HEY! WHO THE HELL ARE YOU?
HOW ARE YOU DOING THAT?
HAS IT REALLY BEEN SO LONG? HAS THE TIME COME UPON US AGAIN SO QUICKLY?
WHAT IS THAT?
BABA YAGA WAS HERE. SHE HAS THE SHARD NOW.
BABA YAGA? WHAT DOES SHE HAVE TO DO WITH ALL THIS? AND WHAT SHARD? SHARD OF WHAT?
IT WON'T BE LONG NOW. SOON THE OTHERS WILL COME. SOON THEY WILL ALL COME. THEY WILL SEARCH THEM OUT.
ARE YOU GOING TO JUST KEEP ON IGNORING ME OR ARE YOU GOING TO LET ME HELP WITH WHATEVER ALL THIS IS?
I FEAR THERE IS VERY LITTLE ANY OF US CAN DO NOW THAT THE WHEELS HAVE BEEN SET INTO MOTION.
BUT WE WILL DO WHAT WE CAN. FOR NOW, THAT IS ALL WE CAN DO.
WHAT CAN I DO?
YOU CAN LISTEN.

"LONG, LONG AGO A CHILD WAS BORN FROM THE UNION OF TWO INCREDIBLY *POWERFUL* HIGHBORN PARENTS. THIS CHILD WAS *UNLIKE* ANY OTHER CHILD WHO HAD EVER BEEN BORN FROM SUCH A JOINING OF LINEAGE IN THAT HE CAME INTO THIS WORLD *WITHOUT* POWERS OF *ANY* KIND.
"IN THE REALM OF MYST, CHILDREN ARE *TRAINED* IN THE USE OF THEIR POWERS FROM A VERY YOUNG AGE. THE BOY HAD NONE BUT WAS *LOVED* BY HIS PARENTS NONETHELESS.
"MANY YEARS PASSED AND THE BOY GREW OLDER. HE LIVED WRAPPED IN THE WARM EMBRACE OF THE LOVE FROM ALL THOSE AROUND HIM AND, FOR A TIME, HE WAS TRULY AS *HAPPY* AS ONE COULD EVER *HOPE* TO BE.
"FOR A TIME."
EEEEEEEGH
"UNTIL HIS DESTINY WOULD FIND HIM AND CHANGE HIS LIFE *FOREVER*."
WHAT! WHAT HAS *HAPPENED* SON?
I *HURT* THE BUNNY. I... I DIDN'T MEAN TO.
*I didn't **mean** to.*
"THE BOY'S NAME WAS HELIOS."

"THAT WAS THE BEGINNING OF HIS LONELY EXISTENCE. AS THE YEARS PASSED HIS POWER CONTINUED TO GROW.
"AN INTENSE INTERNAL FLAME OVER WHICH HE HAD LITTLE TO NO CONTROL.
"WHISPERS OF HIS INABILITY TO CONTROL THE MASSIVE POWERS AT HIS DISPOSAL SPREAD THROUGHOUT THE VILLAGE WHERE HE LIVED AND ALL THOSE WHO CROSSED HIS PATH SHUNNED HIM AS AN OUTCAST AND FREAK OF NATURE.
"NONE WOULD DARE SPEAK THE WORDS, EXCEPT THE MOST FOOLHARDY DRUNKARD. BUT THE BOY HAD LONG LEARNED THE SILENT MEANINGS SPOKEN IN THE STARES OF MAN AND WOMAN ALIKE.
"AS TIME PASSED, THE BOY BECAME A YOUNG MAN. HIS HEART GREW COLD AND EMPTY, BUT THE BITTERNESS WITHIN DID NOT TURN HIM TO EVIL WAYS. THE DESPAIR THAT FILLED HIM DID NOT TURN TO HATE.
"BECAUSE HE KNEW IT WASN'T THEIR FAULT. HIS TOUCH COULD END A LIFE, AND LIVING WITH THAT KNOWLEDGE WAS ENOUGH TO KEEP HIM FROM TURNING DOWN A DARK PATH. AS MUCH AS THE WORLD HAD TAKEN FROM HIM, HE ONLY WISHED TO BE ABLE TO TOUCH ANOTHER.
"HE ONLY WISHED TO B LOVED."

"A WISH THAT *FATE* WOULD *HAPPILY* PROVIDE.

"HELIOS BECAME *ENCHANTED* WITH THE WOMAN'S BEAUTY AND THE *LOVE* THAT HAD SO LONG BEEN *MISSING* FROM HIS HEART ENVELOPED HIM IN WAYS HE HAD NEVER *FELT* BEFORE.
"BUT HELIOS KNEW HE COULD NOT REVEAL HIMSELF TO HER FOR FEAR OF *DESTROYING* THE VERY THING HE SO *ADORED*.

"SO HELIOS SET OUT TO THE FARTHEST REACHES OF THE LAND IN HOPES OF FINDING *SOMETHING* THAT WOULD *ALLOW* HIM TO BE WITH THIS WOMAN WITH WHOM HE HAD BECOME SO TAKEN.
"HIS PARENTS HAD GIFTED HIM WITH A MAGIC *CHARIOT* LONG AGO AND WITH IT HE JOURNEYED TO THE *ONE* PLACE IN ALL OF MYST WHERE THERE MIGHT BE AN *ANSWER* TO THE PROBLEM THAT PLAGUED HIM SO.

"TO THE LAND OF ONE OF THE LAST REMAINING *FROST GIANTS*. THE KING OF A FALLEN RACE... *YMIR*.
"HELIOS HAD LONG HEARD THE STORIES OF THE FROST GIANT WHO DWELLED BEYOND THE FARTHEST REACHES OF MYST AND OF THE MAGICAL BATHING HOLE THE ICE GIANTS USED TO HEAL THEIR WOUNDS FROM BATTLE.

"YMIR, UPON HEARING HIS TALE, TOOK *PITY* ON THE POOR YOUNG MAN AND ALLOWED HIM ACCESS TO THE FROZEN WATERS."

"THE FOLLOWING DAY HELIOS RETURNED TO THE WOMAN AND PRESENTED HER WITH A *GIFT* UNLIKE ANY SHE HAD RECEIVED BEFORE.
"A *ROSE* MADE OF PUREST *ICE* THAT WOULD NEVER MELT, NEVER WILT, AND WOULD STAY BEAUTIFUL FOR *ALL TIME.*
"SENSING HIS PURE AND *KIND* SPIRIT, THE WOMAN GREW TO *LOVE* HELIOS OVER TIME AND, BEFORE LONG, THE TWO WERE *INSEPARABLE.*
"AND FOR THE FIRST TIME SINCE HIS POWERS BECAME HIS *CURSE,* HELIOS WAS *HAPPY.*
"BUT WITH THAT HAPPINESS CAME A *PRICE.* AS THE SUN SET EACH NIGHT HELIOS WOULD BE FORCED TO *RETURN* TO THE FROZEN WATERS TO DOUSE THE BURNING INFERNO THAT *RAGED* WITHIN HIM.
"HIS LOVE WAS GREATLY *HEARTBROKEN* BY THIS -- AS HE LEFT HE *REFUSED* TO TELL HER *WHERE* HE WENT AND *WHY* HE WAS FORCED TO LEAVE HER EACH AND EVERY NIGHT.
"AND ALTHOUGH HIS HEART ACHED TO DO SO, HE KNEW HE COULD NEVER REVEAL THE *TRUTH* OF HIS AFFLICTION AND RISK *LOSING* THE ONE WHO HAD COME TO BE HIS WORLD."

"BUT EVEN WITH THE SECRET BETWEEN THEM, SHE REFUSED TO ***ABANDON*** THEIR LOVE."

FOR SO ***LONG*** I DRIFTED IN THIS WORLD. LOST AND ALONE. EMPTY AND ***DYING*** DAY BY DAY. I LONGED FOR ***DEATH.*** FOR A TIME WHEN MY SOLITUDE MIGHT COME TO AN ***END.*** I HAD COME TO ***ACCEPT*** MY FATE. TO ACCEPT THAT MY LIFE WAS SORROW AND NOTHING ***MORE.*** UNTIL I FOUND ***YOU.***
YOU ***SAVED*** ME. YOU GAVE ME A REASON TO ***BE.*** YOU GAVE ME ***LOVE*** AND FOR THAT I SWEAR BY THE KEEPERS BEYOND I WILL NEVER ALLOW ANY HARM TO ***EVER*** BEFALL YOU.
YOU ARE ***EVERYTHING*** THAT MATTERS AND OUR LOVE WILL BURN LONG AFTER THE SUN IS AN EMPTY, COLD THING.
BUT IF YOU ARE TO LOVE ***ME,*** YOU MUST ***TRUST*** ME. YOU MUST NEVER ASK ME ***WHERE*** IT IS I GO AND ***WHY*** I MUST LEAVE YOU EACH NIGHT.
VERY WELL, MY LOVE.
I WILL GIVE YOU ***EVERYTHING*** YOU DESIRE. ***BE*** EVERYTHING YOU DESIRE BUT PLEASE ALLOW ME THIS ***SINGLE*** RESPITE.

"AND, FOR A TIME, THEY WERE HAPPY.

"FOR A TIME."

"SHE HAD LOVED HIM MORE THAN THE AIR SHE BREATHED, BUT EVEN THAT WAS NOT ENOUGH TO QUELL THE CURIOSITY THAT SEARED HER SOUL.

"AND IT WAS THAT VERY LOVE THAT LEFT HIM BLIND TO WHAT SHE HAD ALWAYS SEEN...

"THAT ALL THE LOV IN THE WORLD IS NOTHING WITHOU TRUST.

"THAT NOTHING CHIPS AWAY AT TRUST MORE THAN A SECRET.
"AND ONCE THAT TRUST IS GONE..."
"IT ALWAYS LEAVES US..."
Helios?

I'm so cold.

WHAT HAPPENED TO THE GIRL?
THE GIRL...

NO. NOT NOW. NOT ALREADY.
COME. WE MUST GO.
WAIT. WHAT ARE YOU TALKING ABOUT?

YOU SAID YOU WISHED TO HELP?
YES, BUT WHERE ARE WE GOING?

HERE.
WHERE ARE WE?
THERE. ON THAT VESSEL. WITHIN IT LIES ANOTHER SHARD. YOU MUST RETRIEVE IT IMMEDIATELY.
I CAN SENSE OTHERS DRAWING NEAR. YOU MUST HURRY.
I DON'T UNDERSTAND. WHY CAN'T YOU JUST FREEZE TIME LIKE YOU DID BACK IN THE CITY AND GET IT YOURSELF.

I ***CANNOT.*** THE SHARD... LIMITS ME. IT LIMITS MY ***POWER.*** CANNOT ***INTERFERE.*** IT IS P TO ***YOU.*** IF THE SHARD FALLS INTO THE ***WRONG*** HANDS...

OKAY. OKAY. BAD ***STUFF*** WILL HAPPEN. I ***GET*** IT.

JUST STAY THERE TILL I GET BACK. YOU STILL HAVE A LOT OF ***EXPLAINING*** TO...

IT'S CLOSE. ***VERY*** CLOSE.

SO CLOSE.

MY MISTRESS HAS ***NEED*** OF YOU...

KRASH

...AND THE ***POWER*** YOU HOLD.

POWER THAT I NOW HOLD.

YOU!
LOOK WHO HAS COME TO PLAY. HELLO, GUARDIAN. WE WOULD LOVE TO STAY AND CHAT...
214

...BUT YOU LOOK LIKE YOU HAVE YOUR HANDS FULL.
HREEEEEEEEEE
THRAAK

BUT DON'T LET THAT STOP YOU.
I'M SURE THE HUMANS WON'T MIND.
DAMN YOU.
COME, MY PET. LET'S LEAVE THE FALSEBLOOD TO HER SILLY HEROICS.

"WE HAVE MUCH BIGGER FISH TO FRY."
ELSEWHERE.
THE WORLD IS A COLD PLACE, AND HE KNOWS THAT VERY WELL. ONCE UPON A TIME, HE HAD A NAME.
EDWARD PEIRCE.

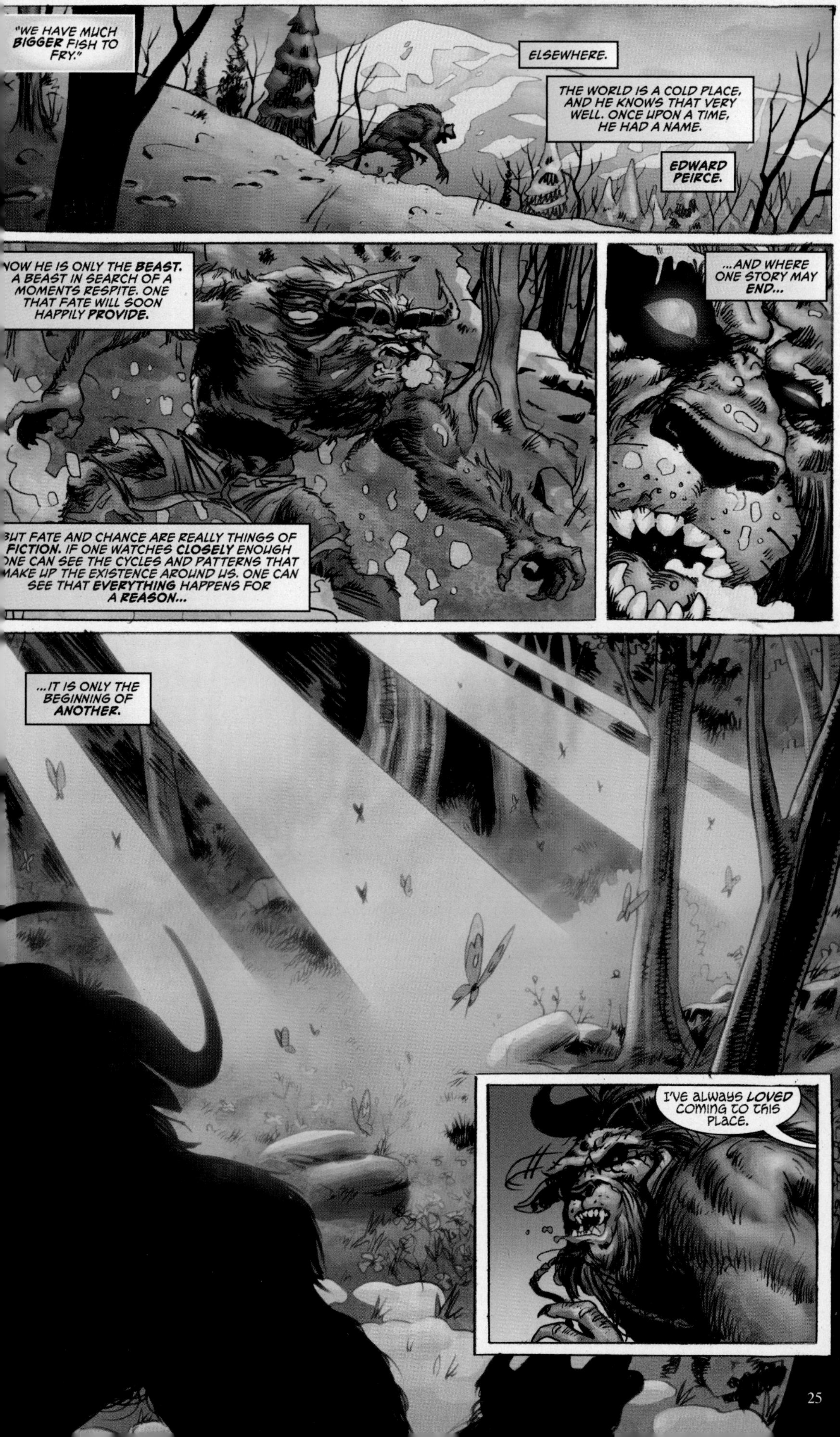

NOW HE IS ONLY THE BEAST. A BEAST IN SEARCH OF A MOMENTS RESPITE. ONE THAT FATE WILL SOON HAPPILY PROVIDE.
BUT FATE AND CHANCE ARE REALLY THINGS OF FICTION. IF ONE WATCHES CLOSELY ENOUGH ONE CAN SEE THE CYCLES AND PATTERNS THAT MAKE UP THE EXISTENCE AROUND US. ONE CAN SEE THAT EVERYTHING HAPPENS FOR A REASON...

...AND WHERE ONE STORY MAY END...

...IT IS ONLY THE BEGINNING OF ANOTHER.

I'VE ALWAYS LOVED COMING TO THIS PLACE.

FOR AS LONG AS I CAN REMEMBER IT'S ALWAYS BEEN A PLACE THAT HAS BROUGHT ME *JOY* AND *PEACE*.
PEACE THAT I CAN OFFER YOU...
MY *BEAUTIFUL* BEAST.
TO BE CONTINUED

# Grimm Fairy Tales™
# Myths & Legends

# Chapter Two:
# The Gathering, Part 2

Story by Raven Gregory, Joe Brusha, and Ralph Tedesco

Written by Raven Gregory • Art by V. Kenneth Marion and Marco Cosentino

Colors by Jeff Balke and Roland Pilcz • Letters by Jim Campbell

I SHOULD HAVE BEEN HERE SOONER.
WE SHOULD HAVE BEEN HERE SOONER.
WE COULD HAVE STOPPED THIS FROM HAPPENING. WHY DIDN'T WE STOP THIS FROM HAPPENING?
IT'S NOT YOUR FAULT.

WE SHOULD HAVE KNOWN. WE SHOULD HAVE BEEN READY.
I CAN'T TAKE MUCH MORE OF THIS MYSTERY CRAP. WHAT THE HELL IS GOING ON THERE?
WHY ARE ERICA, THE SEA WITCH, AND BABA YAGA CHASING STATUES? GIVE ME SOMETHING, DAMNIT.
SIGH
I DON'T EVEN KNOW WHAT TO CALL YOU... WHOEVER YOU ARE.
I AM THE INNOCENT. I AM ONE OF THE FIVE KEEPERS OF THE REALMS OF POWER.
AND WE HAVE MADE A TERRIBLE MISTAKE.
ONE THAT THAT BEGAN LONG AGO... ALLOW ME TO FINISH THE STORY OF HELIOS.

"HELIOS RACED HOME WITH HIS BELOVED IN HIS ARMS. BARELY BREATHING AND SO CLOSE TO DEATH HE PRAYED TO THE GODS ABOVE THAT SHE MIGHT SURVIVE ANOTHER NIGHT.
"FOR THE FIRST TIME IN HIS LIFE HE THOUGHT NOTHING OF HIMSELF AND ONLY OF HER.
"ONLY OF HIS LOVE.

"THE HOURS DRIFTED BY ON SLOW TEDIOUS WINDS THAT SEEMED TO NEVER END. THE SANDS OF TIME PAUSED AND WAITED UNTIL HE THOUGHT HE MIGHT BE DRIVEN INSANE BY THEIR UNSYMPATHETIC TOUCH.

"UNTIL, FINALLY, SHE WOKE. WEAK AND STILL NEAR DEATH, HE CARED FOR HER. AND EVENTUALLY DEATH'S EMBRACE GAVE WAY TO LIFE'S PROMISE OF ANOTHER DAY."

I DREAMED I FOLLOWED YOU. TO THE PLACE YOU WOULD NOT REVEAL TO ME.
I DREAMED I HID IN YOUR CHARIOT AND FLEW AMONG THE CLOUDS TO A PLACE OF SUCH COLD THAT ICE MUST HAVE FELT GREATER WARMTH AMONG THE SNOWSTORMS AND FROZEN TUNDRAS OF THE NORTH THAN I HAD IN MY ICY HIDING PLACE.
BUT AS I FELT MYSELF DRIFTING AWAY INTO A NUMB, UNFEELING PLACE, YOU ARRIVED TO SAVE ME FROM THAT UNMERCIFUL LIMBO.
"AND FOR THE FIRST TIME IN HIS LIFE, HELIOS FELT TRULY HELPLESS AT THE THOUGHT OF WHAT WOULD BECOME OF HIM IF ANY ILL FATE EVER BEFELL HIS BELOVED."

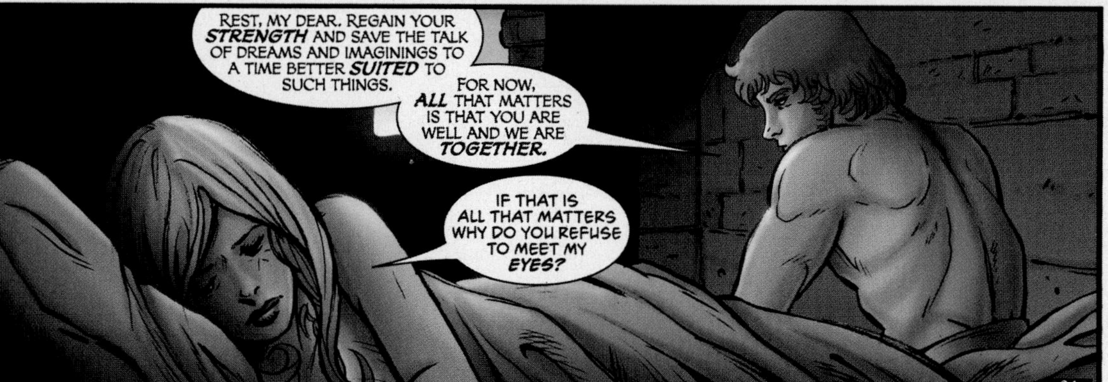
REST, MY DEAR. REGAIN YOUR STRENGTH AND SAVE THE TALK OF DREAMS AND IMAGININGS TO A TIME BETTER SUITED TO SUCH THINGS.
FOR NOW, ALL THAT MATTERS IS THAT YOU ARE WELL AND WE ARE TOGETHER.
IF THAT IS ALL THAT MATTERS WHY DO YOU REFUSE TO MEET MY EYES?

WHAT BURDEN DO YOU CARRY THAT WEIGHS SO HEAVY THAT IT MUST BE YOURS AND YOURS ALONE TO CARRY?
DO YOU DOUBT THE LOVE I HAVE FOR YOU SO MUCH THAT YOU CANNOT BEAR TO UNBURDEN YOURSELF OF IT BUT FOR A MOMENT?
I DO NOT DOUBT OUR LOVE BUT YOU SPEAK OF THINGS YOU CANNOT POSSIBLY KNOW. THERE ARE THINGS BETTER LEFT UNSAID.
IT IS BECAUSE I SO TREASURE OUR LOVE THAT I WOULD DO ANYTHING TO PROTECT YOU FROM THAT WHICH YOU CANNOT POSSIBLY UNDERSTAND.
NO MATTER HOW DARK OR TERRIBLE THE SECRET I WILL ALWAYS LOVE YOU.
BUT YOU WILL NEVER KNOW THAT IF YOU REFUSE TO TRUST IN WHAT WE HAVE.

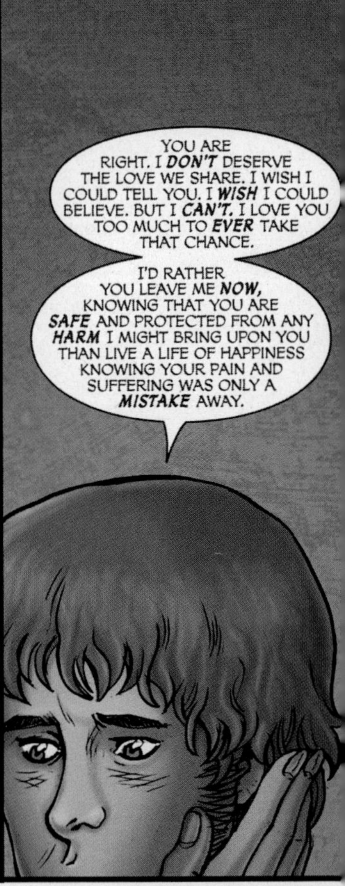
YOU ARE RIGHT. I DON'T DESERVE THE LOVE WE SHARE. I WISH I COULD TELL YOU. I WISH I COULD BELIEVE. BUT I CAN'T. I LOVE YOU TOO MUCH TO EVER TAKE THAT CHANCE.
I'D RATHER YOU LEAVE ME NOW, KNOWING THAT YOU ARE SAFE AND PROTECTED FROM ANY HARM I MIGHT BRING UPON YOU THAN LIVE A LIFE OF HAPPINESS KNOWING YOUR PAIN AND SUFFERING WAS ONLY A MISTAKE AWAY.

AND IF I MUST CHOOSE BETWEEN LIVING A LIFE OF IGNORANCE BUT WRAPPED IN YOUR LOVE I WOULD RATHER BE BLIND THAN EVER SEE THE LIGHT.
MY LOVE...
SHHHHHHH. NO WORDS. NO WORDS AT ALL.

JUST HOLD ME. HOLD ME AND NEVER LET ME GO.

"AND THERE THEY SLEPT, WRAPPED IN EACH OTHER'S ARMS. MORE AT *PEACE* THAN EITHER HAD EVER BEEN.

"IT WAS THE DREAM THEY HAD DESIRED THEIR ENTIRE *LIVES.*

"...THAT WOULD SOON BECOME...
tSSSSSSSSSSS

NOOOOOOoo!

"ONE FROM WHICH HE WOULD ***NEVER*** AWAKE."

"HER DEATH LEFT HIM BROKEN.

"AN EMPTY ***SHELL*** OF WHAT WAS ONCE A MAN, BUT NOW..."

"HIS MIND ***SHATTERED*** BEYOND REPAIR.

"...ONLY ALONE.

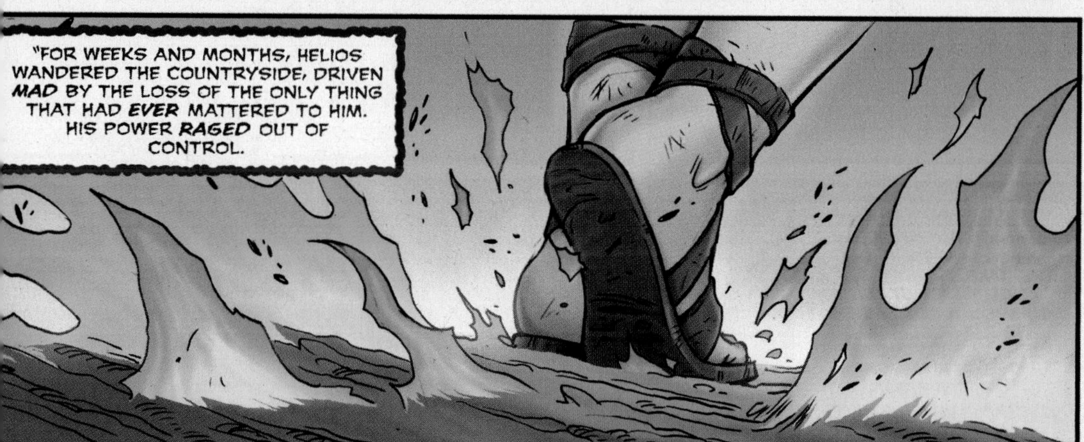
"FOR WEEKS AND MONTHS, HELIOS WANDERED THE COUNTRYSIDE, DRIVEN *MAD* BY THE LOSS OF THE ONLY THING THAT HAD *EVER* MATTERED TO HIM. HIS POWER *RAGED* OUT OF CONTROL.

"THE *FIRE* HE HAD STRUGGLED TO CONTAIN FOR SO LONG WAS *UNLEASHED* UPON THE REALM OF MYST. NO LONGER CONSCIOUS OF HIS OWN ACTIONS, HE BECAME A DESTRUCTIVE FORCE OF *NATURE*...

"...AND EVERYTHING THAT KNEW HIS *TOUCH* WAS BURNED TO *ASH*."

"EVENTUALLY, WORD OF HIS EXISTENCE REACHED THE EARS OF THE *COUNCIL* AND THEY SET OUT TO *CONTAIN* HIS THREAT. REALIZING HE WAS A BEING *WITHOUT* MALICE, THEY CHOSE TO TAKE *MERCY* ON HIS TRAGIC, BROKEN SOUL.

"USING AN ANCIENT MAGIC THAT WAS LONG FORGOTTEN IN THE REALMS, THANE USED A *FORBIDDEN SPELL* TO SUMMON A *PORTAL* THAT WOULD *HOLD* HELIOS' UNHOLY FURY AND KEEP THE REALMS *SAFE* FROM HARM.

"A SPELL THAT COULD ONLY BE USED ONCE A *MILLENNIUM,* WHEN THE STARS ACROSS THE COSMOS ALIGNED ALLOWING FOR THE MOST POWERFUL *PRISON* EVER CREATED TO ONLY BE OPENED MOMENTARILY.
"AND SO IT WAS, THAT WITH HEAVY SYMPATHETIC HEARTS, THE COUNCIL IMPRISONED AN *INNOCENT* BEING IN THE HEART OF THE *SUN*...

"...AND LEFT HIM TO SPEND ALL ETERNITY EVEN MORE *ALONE* THAN EVER BEFORE."

"...AND GIVEN TO THANE'S MOST *LOYAL* COMRADES TO *HIDE* ACROSS THE REALMS.
WITH HELIOS CONTAINED, THE *SUNSTONE OF RA* WAS SHATTERED INTO THREE PIECES...

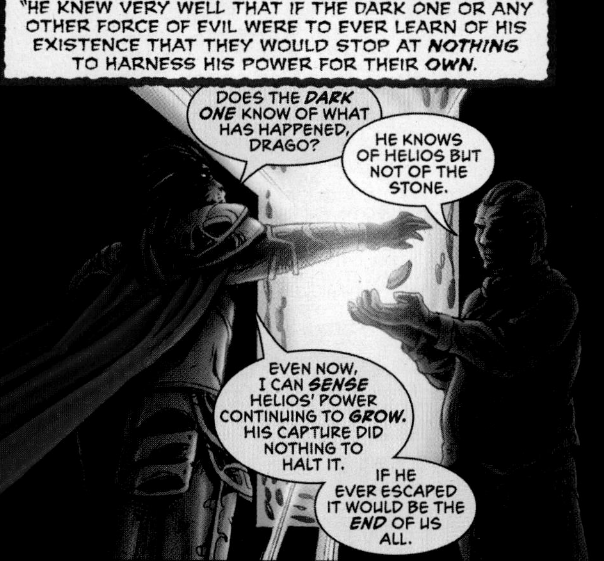
"HE KNEW VERY WELL THAT IF THE DARK ONE OR ANY OTHER FORCE OF EVIL WERE TO EVER LEARN OF HIS EXISTENCE THAT THEY WOULD STOP AT *NOTHING* TO HARNESS HIS POWER FOR THEIR *OWN*.
DOES THE *DARK ONE* KNOW OF WHAT HAS HAPPENED, DRAGO?
HE KNOWS OF HELIOS BUT NOT OF THE STONE.
EVEN NOW, I CAN *SENSE* HELIOS' POWER CONTINUING TO *GROW*. HIS CAPTURE DID NOTHING TO HALT IT.
IF HE EVER ESCAPED IT WOULD BE THE *END* OF US ALL.

MY LOYALTY IS TO YOU AND THE COUNCIL FOREVER, BUT I HAVE A *FAMILY* NOW AND THE DARK ONE IS GROWING *SUSPICIOUS* OF MY BEHAVIOR. IT WON'T BE LONG BEFORE HE LEARNS OF MY TRUE ALLEGIANCE AND *THEN...*
I ASK OF YOU ONE *LAST* TASK.
TAKE THE STONE WITH YOU TO THE *NEXUS* AND HIDE IT WHERE NO ONE WILL *EVER* FIND IT. AND TELL *NO* SOUL WHERE YOU PUT IT. TO DO SO WOULD ONLY PUT THEIR *LIVES* AT RISK. CAN YOU *DO* THIS FOR ME?
YES. I WILL.

THERE IS NO ONE ELSE I CAN *TRUST* WITH THIS.
IT IS NOT MY PLACE.
YOU *KNOW* OF HIS POWER. YOU KNOW WHAT HE IS *CAPABLE* OF. I DOUBT EVEN THE *DREAM EATER* COULD DEVOUR A BEING SUCH AS *THIS*.
WHAT WOULD YOU HAVE ME DO?
WHAT YOU HAVE *ALWAYS* DONE... STAY A *SECRET*.

"BUT THERE ARE PLACES IN THE REALM OF MYST WHERE THERE IS NO SUCH THING AS A SECRET.
"THIS IS SUCH A PLACE."
"HERE, A SECRET ORDER OF GIFTED HOLY MEN AND WOMEN RECORD THE EVER CONSTANT FLOW OF HISTORY. THE PAST, PRESENT AND FUTURE ARE EVER AND ALWAYS REVEALED TO THEIR ALL SEEING EYES.
"EVEN TO THOSE EYES NOT MEANT TO SEE."
MOTHER?
BABA? WHAT ARE YOU DOING STILL AWAKE?
I COULDN'T SLEEP.
...
IS IT THE DREAMS AGAIN?
IT'S OKAY, MY DEAR. THIS IS ALL JUST A PART OF GROWING UP. THERE ARE FEW AS GIFTED AS YOU.
AS IT IS YOUR GIFT IT WILL ALSO BE YOUR BURDEN. THE VISIONS ARE A SIGN OF THAT. SOON YOU WILL JOIN ME AND THE OTHERS IN RECORDING ALL THAT OCCURS IN THE FOUR REALMS OF POWER.
I'M SCARED.
NONSENSE. THERE IS NOTHING TO BE AFRAID...
...NO. THIS... THIS CAN'T BE HERE.
WHAT IS IT, MOTHER? WHAT'S WRONG?
WE MUST SUMMON THE COUNCIL. IMMEDIATELY.

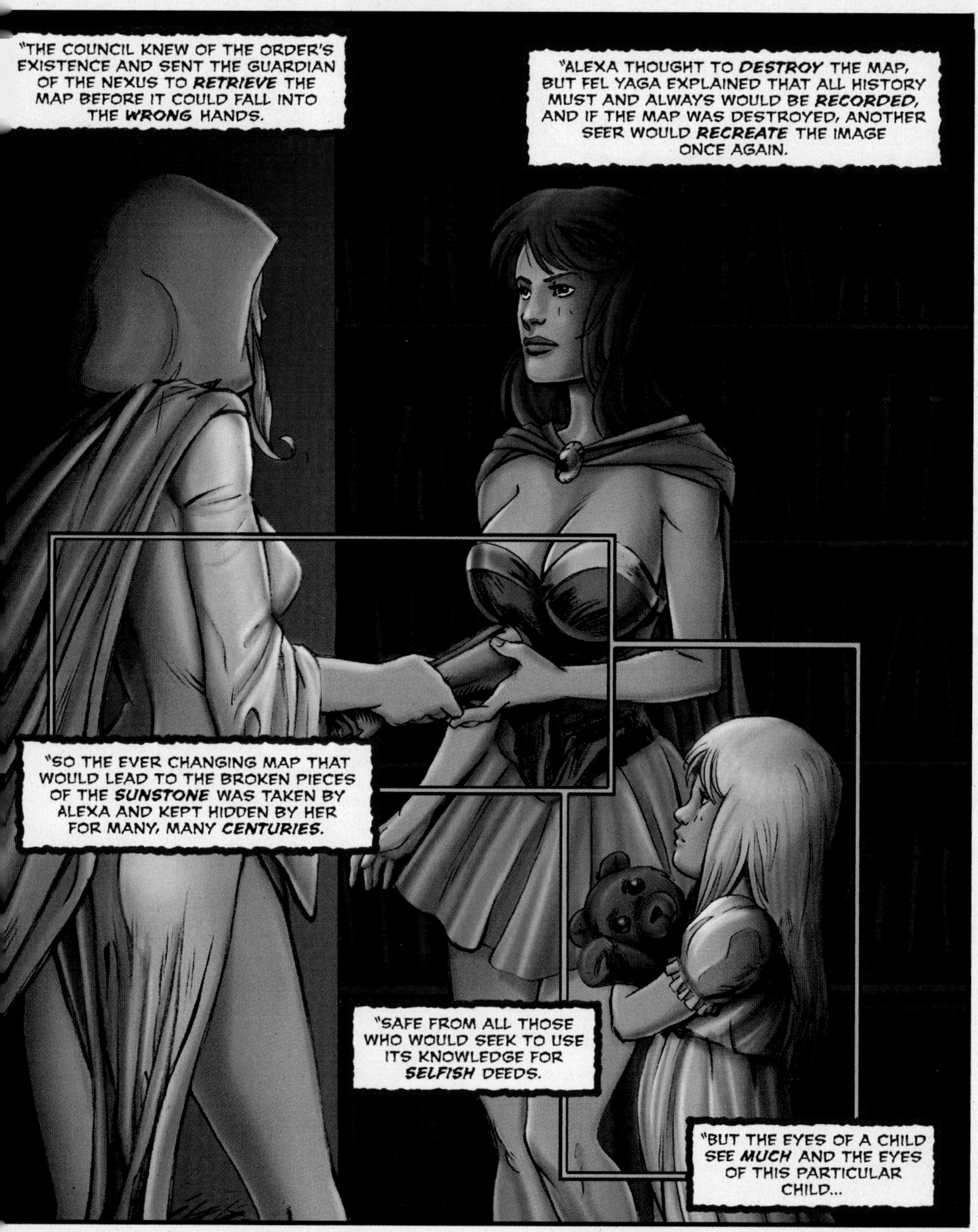

"THE COUNCIL KNEW OF THE ORDER'S EXISTENCE AND SENT THE GUARDIAN OF THE NEXUS TO ***RETRIEVE*** THE MAP BEFORE IT COULD FALL INTO THE ***WRONG*** HANDS.

"ALEXA THOUGHT TO ***DESTROY*** THE MAP, BUT FEL YAGA EXPLAINED THAT ALL HISTORY MUST AND ALWAYS WOULD BE ***RECORDED,*** AND IF THE MAP WAS DESTROYED, ANOTHER SEER WOULD ***RECREATE*** THE IMAGE ONCE AGAIN.

"SO THE EVER CHANGING MAP THAT WOULD LEAD TO THE BROKEN PIECES OF THE ***SUNSTONE*** WAS TAKEN BY ALEXA AND KEPT HIDDEN BY HER FOR MANY, MANY ***CENTURIES.***

"SAFE FROM ALL THOSE WHO WOULD SEEK TO USE ITS KNOWLEDGE FOR ***SELFISH*** DEEDS.

"BUT THE EYES OF A CHILD SEE ***MUCH*** AND THE EYES OF THIS PARTICULAR CHILD...

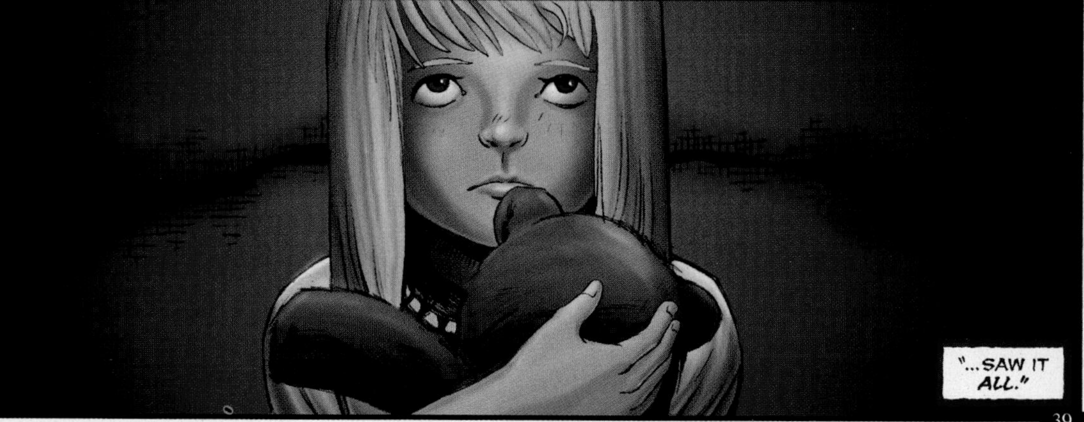

SO BABA YAGA WAS THERE? SHE SAW THE MAP CREATED. SHE KNOWS IT EXISTS.
NO. THE MAP IS SAFE. SHE HAS NO WAY TO SENSE ITS PRESENCE.
THEN HOW DID SHE FIND THE FIRST PIECE? HOW DID THE SEA WITCH FIND THE SECOND? WHAT HAPPENS IF ONE OF THEM FINDS THE THIRD?
I DO NOT KNOW. THE ALIGNMENT IS ALMOST UPON US AGAIN. IT PREVENTS ME FROM SEEING THE TRUTH.
BUT IF EITHER OF THEM FIND THE THIRD PIECE OR THE MAP IT WOULD POSE A GRAVE DANGER TO ALL LIFE AS WE KNOW IT.
THEN WE HAVE TO GET TO THE PIECES FIRST.
I CANNOT SENSE THE PIECES THAT HAVE ALREADY BEEN CAPTURED AND THE LAST PIECE REMAINS HIDDEN TO ME.
THEN WHAT ABOUT THE MAP?
IT'S SAFE.
BUT CAN'T WE USE THE MAP TO FIND THE MISSING PIECE AND KEEP THE BAD GUYS FROM GETTING IT?
THERE IS SOME MERIT TO YOUR IDEA.
SO WHERE IS IT?
IT IS IN THE ONE PLACE WHERE EVIL CANNOT VENTURE. THE INNER SANCTUM OF THE NEXUS. THE SEALS THAT PROTECT THAT PLACE ARE IMPOSSIBLE TO PENETRATE.
THE ONLY WAY ANY BEING OF ILL MOTIVE COULD EVER SENSE THAT PLACE WOULD BE IF A GUARDIAN INVITED THEM IN AND WEAKENED THE BARRIER.*
OH, NO.
*Editor's Note: Which is exactly what happened in Dream Eater Part 3

THE INNER SANCTUM OF THE NEXUS.
WHERE ARE YOU HIDING?
I FELT YOU THE LAST TIME I WAS HERE. IF NOT FOR THE DREAM EATER'S INTERFERENCE YOU WOULD HAVE BEEN MINE ALREADY.
BUT THAT WAS THEN...
...AND THIS IS NOW.
THERE SHE IS.
WHO...?

Ah, IF IT ISN'T MY FAVORITE LITTLE FALSEBLOOD COME TO SAVE THE DAY, ONCE AGAIN.
PUT IT DOWN, BABA. THERE'S NO WAY ON EARTH I'M LETTING YOU LEAVE HERE ALIVE WITH THAT THING.
Oh, SAMANTHA, I'M HURT. I WAS SO HOPING WE MIGHT HAVE OURSELVES ANOTHER LITTLE TEAM UP AGAIN. THE LAST TIME WAS SO MUCH... FUN...
INTERESTING. YOUR FRIEND... SHE'S BLANK. AS IF SHE'S NOT THERE. I'VE FELT THIS BEFORE. MANY TIMES OVER THE CENTURIES. MISSING PIECES OF THE STORY.
MY MOTHER AND OTHER SEERS AS WELL. WE COULD NEVER TELL WHAT IT WAS... BUT ALL THIS TIME... IT WAS YOU.
WHAT ARE YOU, MYSTERY GIRL?
I WON'T ASK YOU AGAIN. PUT IT DOWN OR I'LL DESTROY THE MAP MYSELF AND YOU ALONG WITH IT.
NO. YOU CAN'T. WE CAN'T RISK ANOTHER SEER HAVING THE MAP REVEALED TO THEM.
DESTROYING IT WOULD JUST PUT THE MAP IN UNKNOWN HANDS.

GOOD TO KNOW. WELL, I'D LOVE TO STAY AND CHAT BUT THE STARS IN THE SKIES WILL SOON BE RIGHT AND IF I'M GOING TO FIND THE LAST PIECE OF SUNSTONE I SHOULD REALLY BE ON MY WAY.
YOU'RE NOT GOING ANYWHERE.
SILLY CHILD. WHEN WILL YOU EVER LEARN?
I'VE ALWAYS KNOWN HOW THIS ALL ENDS. I'LL ALWAYS BE ONE STEP AHEAD OF YOU AND YOU'LL ALWAYS BE ONE SECOND TOO LATE.
NO!

OOOFTHH!
NOT AGAIN.
SHE'S GONE.
ANY IDEA WHERE?
NO.
I CAN'T SENSE HER, EITHER. MUST BE THAT DAMN SPELL SHE USED THE LAST TIME I MET HER.
SO WHAT DO WE DO NOW?
I...I DON'T KNOW.
AT LEAST YOU STILL HAVE THE KEY. YOU DO HAVE THE KEY STILL?
YES.
THEN AS LONG AS NO ONE KNOWS ABOUT THAT WE HAVE A CHANCE BUT WE BETTER HURRY AND FIND THAT LAST PIECE WHERE EVER IT IS...
...AND WE BETTER FIND IT FAST.

ELSEWHERE--
AMAZING. SOMETHING SO SMALL YET SO POWERFUL.
JUST LIKE I SAID.
DID YOU HAVE ANY PROBLEMS RETRIEVING IT?
THE FALSEBLOOD WAS THERE AGAIN.
SHE IS PROVING TO BE QUITE AN ANNOYANCE. EVENTUALLY, SHE WILL HAVE TO BE DEALT WITH.
THE SOONER THE BETTER.
HMMMMM. INTERESTING. WHAT OF THE DARK ONE? DOES HE KNOW WHO STOLE THE PIECES FROM HIM?
YES. HE KNOWS.
PERFECT.
AND WHAT OF YOU? DID YOU RETRIEVE YOUR PIECE OF THE STONE? WHAT OF THE MAP?
YES. I HAVE THE STONE AND THE MAP. THE FALSEBLOOD WAS THERE, AS WELL. BUT THERE WAS ALSO SOMEONE ELSE. A NEW PLAYER IN THE GAME.
BETTER THAN PERFECT.
HE HAD NO IDEA I KNEW HE HAD FOUND THOSE TWO PIECES OF THE STONE.

SO NOW THAT YOU HAVE BROUGHT ME NOT ONLY YOUR PIECE BUT THE MAP AS WELL, IS THERE ANY REASON WHY I SHOULDN'T JUST KILL YOU NOW?
KNOW THAT I HAVE NO PROBLEM DESTROYING YOU WHERE YOU STAND IF YOU EVEN THINK TO BETRAY ME.
THE RITUAL IS ANCIENT AND THERE ARE NONE WHO KNOW THE FORBIDDEN CRAFT BUT I. IF YOU KILL ME, ALL YOU HAVE ARE TWO PIECES OF STONE AND A SCRAP OF PAPER.
THE THOUGHT HADN'T EVEN CROSSED MY MIND.
YOU NEVER DID TELL ME HOW THE DARK ONE ACQUIRED THE PIECES TO BEGIN WITH.
ONE WAS GIVEN TO HIM BY A POWERFUL WIZARD WHO HAD HAD ENOUGH OF THE COUNCIL'S INTERFERENCE IN HIS PERSONAL MATTERS.
AND THE OTHER?
THE OTHER WAS TAKEN FROM THE PREVIOUS GUARDIAN OF THE NEXUS.
"AFTER SHANG, FEARING IT FALLING INTO THE WRONG HANDS, GAVE IT TO HER FOR SAFE KEEPING.
"BUT HE WAS UNAWARE OF THE DARK ONE'S MINIONS WATCHING FROM THE SHADOWS.*
ONE FINAL PIECE REMAINS. ONCE WE FIND IT AND THE STARS ALIGN WE WILL HAVE ACCESS TO THE MOST POWERFUL HIGHBORN IN ALL THE FOUR REALMS. THERE WILL BE NOTHING THAT CAN STOP US.
HE WAS RIGHT ABOUT ONE THING. SOON WE WILL HAVE THE FINAL PIECE AND NOTHING IN THE WORLD WILL STAND IN THE WAY OF MY VENGEANCE.
AND ONCE THE DARK ONE IS DESTROYED THERE WILL BE NOTHING LEFT TO STAND IN OUR WAY FROM RULING THE WORLD ONCE AND FOR ALL.
*Editor's Note: See Grimm Fairy Tales #42

NEW YORK CITY--
THIS HAS ALWAYS BEEN MY FAVORITE CITY. NOT ANOTHER ONE LIKE IT.
A SHAME THE NATIVES TEND TO KEEP IT SUCH A MESS.
BUT WE'LL HELP THEM CLEAN IT UP NOW, WON'T WE?

THERE, AT THE TOP. THAT'S WHERE DRAGO HID IT.
MUST YOU KILL THEM ALL? HAVEN'T YOU EVER HEARD OF SAVING SOMETHING FOR DESSERT?
VERY CLEVER, DRAGO. BUT YOUR PETTY SPELL WILL NOT KEEP ME FROM WHAT IS MINE.
REVEAL YOURSELF.
IT'S SUCH A SHAME DRAGO COULDN'T BE HERE TO SEE HOW HORRIBLY HE FAILED HIS PRECIOUS COUNCIL.
THEY'D BE ASHAMED TO LEARN HOW EASILY AN INNOCENT MAIDEN COULD SEDUCE ONE OF THEIR MOST TRUSTED ALLIES INTO REVEALING THE MOST INTIMATE OF DETAILS.
AND ALL IT TOOK WAS A KISS.

I have waited SO long for this moment. Ever since I was banished by the council I KNEW the day of my REVENGE would come.
And now that the council is no more, with the power of HELIOS at my disposal, there will be NOTHING that will stop me from RULING this world once again.
Come, my beast. There is still MUCH we must do. Absolute power awaits.

"LET'S NOT KEEP IT WAITING."
I AM SURROUNDED BY FOOLS. ALL FOOLS.
FOOLS THAT NOT ONLY CANNOT PROTECT ONE PIECE OF THE SUNSTONE, BUT FOOLS WHO CANNOT PROTECT THE OTHER PIECE, EITHER.

HMMMM. BUT WHAT IS THIS?
MAYBE ALL IS NOT LOST AFTER ALL.

WHAT DO WE HAVE HERE?
GINA AND HANK TACKLE THE MYSTERIES OF THE SUPERNATURAL THAT NO ONE ELSE CAN. GET READY FOR THE RIDE OF YOUR LIFE IN "SEARCHING FOR THE SUPERNATURAL."

THIS MAY BEAR WATCHING.

YOU NEVER KNOW WHAT ELSE IS OUT THERE.
NOT THE END.

# Grimm Fairy Tales™
# Myths & Legends

# Chapter Three: The Summoning, Part 1

Story by Raven Gregory, Joe Brusha, Ralph Tedesco, and Troy Brownfield

Written by Troy Brownfield and Raven Gregory • Art by Josh Hood

Colors by Geraldo Filho • Letters by Jim Campbell

FOR ALL THAT I AM, I AM FEARED. FOR ALL THAT I DO, I AM HATED.
AND EVER HAVE I GIVEN THEM REASON. FEW MORE THAN HER. I SWORE THAT I WOULD COME FOR HER.
OUR ENMITY RUNS DEEP, A CLASSIC HATRED. THIS NIGHT, IT PUTS ME IN MIND OF THE ILIAD.
IT BEGINS, "SING, GODDESS, OF THE ANGER OF THE MAN
I'M NO LONGER A MAN. BUT I AM DEFINITELY ANGRY.

I REMEMBER LITTLE BEFORE I LED THE HORDE IN THAT TIME BEFORE THE COUNCIL FORMED.
WE WERE AS GODS TO THE PEASANTRY. WE BURNED, WE LOOTED. WE TOOK THEIR CROPS AND THEIR HORSES AND THEIR WOMEN.
I PUT OTHER CAPTAINS AND KINGS UNDER THE SWORD, AND MY ARMY GREW.

I KNEW THE VALUE OF POWER. AND I KNEW THAT GREATER POWERS HAD TO BE APPEASED.
THE MOUNTAIN HAD ALWAYS BEEN A PLACE OF SACRIFICE.
AND IN ORDER TO MAINTAIN MY DOMINATION...
THE MOUNTAIN HAD TO BE FED.

UNFORTUNATELY, ONE OF MY MEN HAD GROWN DISSATISFIED AT THIS PRACTICE.
TO CHALLENGE ME IN THIS MOST EVIL OF PLACES.
HIS NAME WAS SHANG.
I WAS SUPREMELY CONFIDENT. I WAS A LEADER OF MEN, AND HE WAS PART OF THE RABBLE, ABSORBED FROM MY CONQUESTS

CLEARLY, I WAS **MISTAKEN.**

SHANG **BESTED** ME AND **DISPERSED** THE HORDE. IT WAS ONE HUMILIATION THAT WOULD TAKE ME **CENTURIES** TO OVERCOME.

ONE TOO MANY.

EVENTUALLY, **CORRUPTION** AND **HATRED** CAME, DRIVEN BY **FEAR**. FEAR THAT THE POWER IN ME COMBINED WITH THE POWER OF THAT PLACE WOULD UNLEASH SOMETHING **HORRIBLE** UPON MYST.

THEY WOULD NOT HAVE ME BE THE CORRUPTING TOXIN THAT THE **JABBERWOCKY** WAS IN **WONDERLAND**.

THEY **DREW** UPON THE POWER OF THAT PLACE. THEY CONDENSED ALL OF ITS THREATENING **EVIL**, ALL OF ITS LINGERING **POWER**...

... AND PUSHED IT INTO ONE CONTAINER, ONE VESSEL OF POWER AND CORRUPTION AND HATRED AND FIRE.

AND I WAS
REBORN.

MORRIGAN?
YES?
CINDY. HANK. GINA. PATRICIA. *BRING* THEM.
SKASSH

I TIRE... OF THE STENCH OF FAILURE. OVER AND OVER, I FIND MY PEOPLE UNABLE TO BRING ME THE PIECES OF THE SUNSTONE OF RA.
CINDY
HANK
MORRIGAN
GINA
PATRICIA
THE DARK ONE
FOR MY PART, I--
WILL NOT SPEAK.
FORTUNATELY, WE WILL HAVE FURTHER ASSISTANCE. HANK AND GINA RECENTLY DISCOVERED THEIR GIFTS.
HIS TELEKINESIS AND HER PYROKINETICS SHOULD PROVE VALUABLE.
AND DEAR PATRICIA, HER DAUGHTER LOST DUE TO THE MACHINATIONS OF SELA,* HAS BEEN HONING HER ARBOREAL TALENT FOR SOME TIME.
*See Grimm Fairy Tales #17
ARBOREAL? SHE WHAT -- CONTROLS PLANTS?
IT IS MORE IMPRESSIVE THAN YOU MIGHT BELIEVE, HANK. IF YOU RECALL, IT WASN'T SO LONG AGO THAT YOU COULD DO NOTHING.

EVEN NOW, BABA YAGA MOVES TOWARD THE SUMMONING. THIS WILL NOT OCCUR IF IT DOES NOT OCCUR WITHIN MY CONTROL. EVEN NOW, I HAVE OTHER PLAYERS IN PLAY.
BABA YAGA DOESN'T TRUST ANYONE. FORGET YOUR PLAYERS. WE SHOULD FIND HER NOW.
SO EAGER TO RUSH IN, SO SOON AFTER BEING BESTED BY SELA?
OH, I HAVEN'T FORGOTTEN THAT; HER TIME WILL COME.
AS FOR BABA YAGA, EVEN IF SHE DOES USE YOUR PEOPLE TO HELP HER, SHE'S PROVEN MORE THAN CAPABLE OF ESCAPING BETRAYAL EVEN IF SHE MAKES THE MISTAKE OF TRUSTING THEM.
MY DEAR, THE ONLY DIFFERENCE BETWEEN BEING TRUSTING OR NOT IS THAT YOU'RE A LITTLE LESS SURPRISED WHEN THEY STAB YOU IN THE BACK. THE ONLY DRAWBACK TO BACKSTABBING BABA YAGA, CINDY?
YES?
IT MAKES IT HARDER TO SEE THE LOOK ON HER FACE.

I AM CALLED THE *INNOCENT*. AND YET, THERE ARE TIMES WHEN I CONSIDER THAT ALL OF THE THINGS THAT I HAVE SEEN MAKE ME *ANYTHING* BUT THAT.
THE CONCRETE CANYONS OF THIS CITY PUT ME IN MIND OF A *DIFFERENT* CHASM. AND A *FALL*.
WHY DO WE DO *NOTHING?* TOO *MUCH* IS PLACED UPON *SELA*.

IT IS NOT MEANT FOR US TO ACT.
THE OTHERS ACT. AND UNSPEAKABLE HORRORS EMERGE.
THE DARK ONE? YES, THIS IS TRUE.
THE HUMANS HAVE LONG RECOGNIZED THAT THE ONLY NECESSITY FOR EVIL TO TRIUMPH IS A LACK OF ACTION ON THE PART OF THE GOOD.
AND THE TIME MAY COME THAT YOU DECIDE TO ACT. BUT I MAINTAIN THAT IT IS NOT OUR PLACE.
IT. IS. TIME.

"LONG HAVE I WAITED, AND NOW..."
I WILL HAVE MY REVENGE.

ALL IS NEARLY READY, MISTRESS.
EXCELLENT, MY LOYAL CAPTAIN. EXPECT ***GUESTS***.

I SEE THEY'VE ARRIVED. CAPTAIN, FETCH THE LADIES SOME WATER.
I APPRECIATE THE GESTURE, PARTICULARLY SINCE YOU'VE BROUGHT US TO THIS MOST INHOSPITABLE OF PLACES.
YOU KNOW AS WELL AS I THAT THE MAGICK IS ABOUT MAKING CHANGES IN FORCES AND ENERGY, THE FABRIC OF WORLDS AND LIFE.
HOSPITABLE HAS LITTLE TO DO WITH IT. OUR PRIZE BEGINS THERE.
WHAT IS THAT?
IT'S BEEN CALLED MANY THINGS. GATES OF HELL, HELL'S DOOR, THE GIANT FIRE CRATER OF DARVAZA ...
YEARS AGO, MEN FOOLISHLY TRIED TO IGNITE THE NATURAL GAS IN THE FISSURE TO BURN IT OFF. AND IT NEVER STOPPED BURNING. EFFORTS WERE MADE TO SEAL IT, BUT WE TOOK CARE OF THAT.
THAT TEXT THAT YOU FOUND... "NEVER-ENDING FIRE, BURNING FROM THE EARTH ..."
EXACTLY. THIS IS IT. THIS IS THE PLACE OF THE SUMMONING.

AREN'T WE STILL SHORT A PIECE?
YES, LITTLE FISH. BUT IT'S IN THE HANDS OF ALLIES AND ON THE WAY HERE NOW.
ONCE WE HAVE THE PIECES, IT WILL BE A SIMPLE MATTER FOR ALL OF US TO RETRIEVE THE KEY. AND THEN...
"WE'LL ENACT THE RITUAL, AND WE'LL FREE HELIOS FROM HIS INFERNAL PRISON IN THE SUN."

ONCE WE HAVE HIM HERE, WE WILL AIM HIM AT THE DARK ONE...
"...AND FIRE."
AAAARGH

HAHAHA HAHA!
MILADY!
WHAT IS IT? SPEAK!
MILADY! SOME... THING... HAS ARRIVED.

OH, MY GOD.
INTERESTING...
I SEE THAT THE ARRIVAL OF MY LAST GUEST IS IMMINENT.
FINALLY.

BEGIN THE FINAL PREPARATIONS! ON MY COMMAND, BE PREPARED TO SLAUGHTER THE GOATS. HAVE EVERYTHING READY.
AS YOU WISH.
REVENGE, ESEMERELDA. REVENGE AND POWER.
THIS WILL TRULY BE SOMETHING TO SEE.
IT SURELY WILL.
YOU!

VENUS!
WHO ELSE? NOW, GIRLS... WHO WANTS TO START A FIRE?
TO BE CONTINUED!

# Chapter Four: The Summoning, Part 2

Story by Raven Gregory, Joe Brusha, Ralph Tedesco, and Troy Brownfield

Written by Troy Brownfield and Raven Gregory • Art by Tony Donley

Colors by Jason Embury • Letters by Jim Campbell

MY NAME IS SAMANTHA. AND I AM A FAILURE.
I'VE TRIED TO SAVE PEOPLE FROM UNSPEAKABLE FATES. I'VE BEEN A GUARDIAN OF THE NEXUS THAT WE CALL EARTH. ACCORDING TO SOME, I'VE BEEN A HERO.
AND I CAN'T HELP BUT FEEL LIKE I'VE BEEN NOTHING BUT TERRIBLE AT ANY OF IT.

SO WHAT ARE WE SUPPOSED TO DO?
WHAT YOU CAN.
IT'S EASY FOR YOU TO SAY THAT. LOOK AT THIS! I'VE DONE WHAT I CAN OVER AND OVER.
I'VE LOST PEOPLE THAT I WAS SUPPOSED TO SAVE. WE LOST SHANG. WE DON'T EVEN KNOW HOW TO FIND BABA YAGA.
YOU WILL DO WHAT YOU CAN, BECAUSE YOU ARE THE GUARDIAN.
THAT IS TRULY, INCREDIBLY NAÏVE.
NOT NAIVETY. HOPE. HOPE IS THE BENEFIT OF INNOCENCE.
A BIGGER BENEFIT WOULD BE A WAY TO FIND BABA YAGA.

SAMANTHA?
GIVE ME A MINUTE. I'M *THINKING.*
SOMETHING YOU SAID... WHEN I ARRIVED, YOU TOLD ME THAT BABA YAGA WAS GOING TO ASSEMBLE THE STONE.
BUT THE STATUE OF LIBERTY... THAT WAS *VENUS.*
YES.
THEY'RE ALL *TOGETHER.* BABA YAGA. VENUS. THE SEA WITCH.
THIS IS TOO *BIG* FOR THE TWO OF US. BABA YAGA HELD US OFF IN THE INNER SANCTUM BY *HERSELF.*

ALL ALONG, I'VE TRIED TO BE THE BEST, AND I'VE FAILED. I DON'T WANT TO BE A FAILURE, BUT...
YES?
THERE SHOULDN'T BE ANY SHAME IN ADMITTING THAT SOMEONE DOES THE JOB BETTER THAN YOU.
PART OF BEING THE GUARDIAN SHOULD BE KNOWING WHEN YOU HAVE TO TAKE EXTRAORDINARY MEASURES.
SHE'S ON A PATH OF HER CHOOSING. I'M NOT SURE THAT SHE WOULD COME.
SHE'LL COME. BECAUSE NO ONE ELSE UNDERSTANDS WHAT IT MEANS, AND WHAT IT COSTS, TO BE THE GUARDIAN LIKE SHE DOES.

TURKMENISTAN. BABA YAGA HAS GATHERED HER ALLIES AND THE PIECES OF THE SUNSTONE HERE.
IT IS NOT GOING SMOOTHLY.
THE SEA WITCH
BABA YAGA
VENUS
THE BEAST
ERICA! KILL VENUS!
ERICA

NO! YOU DON'T KNOW WHAT SHE HAS DONE...

GRRRRRRRRRR
WON'T BACK DOWN?

FINE.

NEITHER KNOWS IT, BUT THE MERMAID AND THE BEAST HAVE MUCH IN COMMON. THEY'VE BOTH BEEN BETRAYED IN LIFE.
THEY'VE EACH BECOME THE SERVANT OF POWERFUL, EVEN DESPERATE, WOMEN.
AND WHEN THE TIME IS RIGHT, THEIR MONSTERS COME OUT.
ERICA! KILL THE BEAST!
NO, DAMN IT!
STOP!

RAARGGG

IF ONLY I COULD WATCH YOU GAG AND SPUTTER FOR LIFE AS I CHOKED THE LAST BREATH OUT OF YOU...
DO SHUT UP...

I'LL FIND A WAY AROUND THAT CURSE, AND WHEN I DO...

NO!

ENOUGH!

YOU KNOW THE CYCLOPS' EYE. YOU KNOW HOW SERIOUS I AM ABOUT DESTROYING THE DARK ONE. I WILL NOT LET YOUR PERSONAL VENDETTA RUIN THIS FOR ANY OF US.
YOU DON'T KNOW--
OF COURSE I KNOW WHAT SHE DID TO YOU. IT CAN WAIT. I KNOW THAT I COULD KILL YOU ALL RIGHT HERE AND PERFORM THE SUMMONING MYSELF.
BUT I WON'T.

BECAUSE YOU KNOW THAT THIS WILL BE EASIER IF WE ALL WORK TOGETHER.
YES. AND IF YOU ARE THROUGH FOR THE MOMENT, I HAVE AN ERRAND THAT THE THREE OF US CAN ATTEND.
THAT IS, IF ALL OF YOUR PETS CAN PLAY NICELY.

I WILL PUT IT ASIDE. REMOVING THE DARK ONE BENEFITS ALL.
I TOLD YOU BEFORE THAT I WOULD AID YOU. WHAT'S THE ERRAND?

TRUST ME. YOU'RE GOING TO LOVE IT.

THANK YOU FOR AGREEING TO MEET THEM HERE.
THIS PLACE HAS NO SIGNIFICANCE THAT I AM AWARE OF.
I WAS JUST TIRED OF LOOKING AT THE WRECKAGE OF A CITY THAT I COULDN'T DO ANYTHING TO *SAVE.*
THEY'RE HERE.
WAIT... THAT DOESN'T...
*SWEET JESUS!*

*SAMANTHA!*
SHRAAAK

I CAN'T FEEL MY *POWER!* WHAT'S *HAPPENING?!*

TO THE LITTLE ONE THAT YOU SAW THIS SPELL ON SINBAD'S BOAT?
ANTI-MAGIC...
THAT'S RIGHT, LITTLE GUARDIAN. SO DON'T TRY ANYTHING. IT JUST WON'T WORK.
AND MY SPELL OF BINDING IS ENOUGH FOR YOU RIGHT NOW.
SHE HAS THE KEY ON HER. PUT HER TO SLEEP AND WE'LL TAKE HER WITH US.
NO, YOU WON'T!

Oh, CHILD.

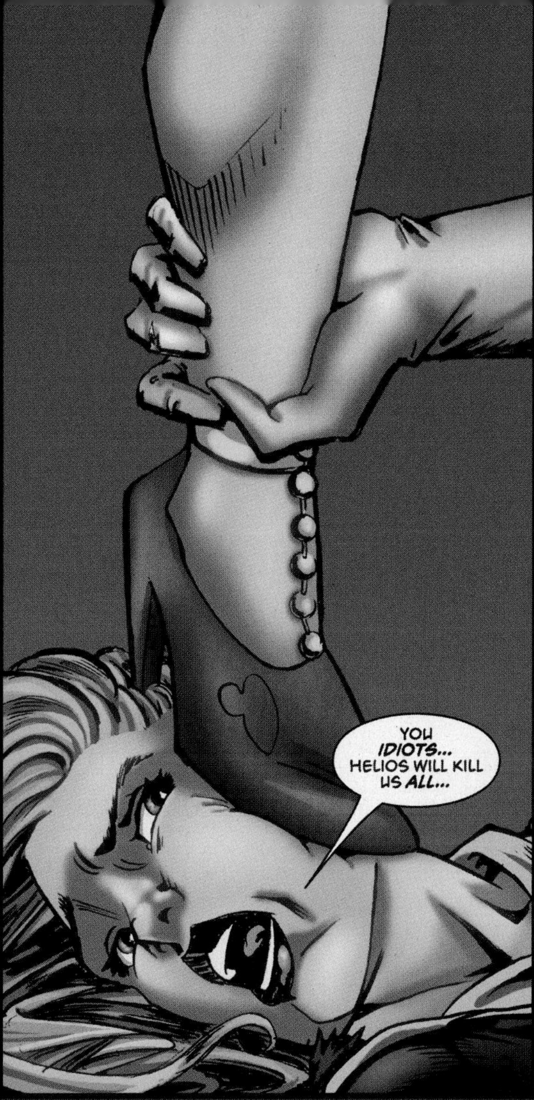

YOU *IDIOTS...* HELIOS WILL KILL US *ALL...*

DO WE *NEED* THIS ONE?

I MAY HAVE TO TOLERATE *YOU*, BUT I DON'T RECALL NEEDING A *GUARDIAN* AT ALL.

SKTCH
SHKK
THWAM

HUDD
VENUS? ESMERALDA? IT'S TIME THIS WAS *OVER.*
YOU'RE DAMN RIGHT ABOUT *THAT.*

SELA MATHERS
HOW MANY WAYS CAN I SAY, "STEP AWAY FROM MY GIRLS?"
MARCUS JENKINS
BRITNEY WATERS

PROTECT OUR PEOPLE!
MOVE!

DAMN YOU, SELA!
DAMN ME? YOU PLAN TO RELEASE A MONSTER FROM THE SUN AND I'M THE PROBLEM?

CALL OFF YOUR DOGS, GIRL!
THEY DON'T LIKE TO BE CALLED DOGS. AND THEY REALLY DON'T LIKE YOU.

YOU HAVE A WARRIOR'S HEART; I CAN TELL. WHAT ON EARTH ARE YOU DOING WITH SELA?
SHE SAYS THINGS THAT MAKE SENSE TO ME.
SUCH AS?

"IF WE RUN INTO A BLONDE BITCH NAMED VENUS, HIT HER WITH SOMETHING HEAVY."
THWAK

MARCUS! A LITTLE HELP!

SHRRIP
YOU'RE NEXT, CHILD!
EEEEYAARRRGGH!
SHAAAK
DOWN!

YOU SHOULD BE HELPING ME!
YOU SHOULD BE IN A COUPLE OF PIECES.

BABA YAGA, I AM NO LONGER LOVING THIS ERRAND. ESMERALDA! GRAB THE INNOCENT!
SHZAAAAK

DAMN IT!

Sela...
OH, MY GOD. SWEETIE, WHAT DID THEY DO TO YOU?

I'M SORRY, SELA. SHE WAS TOO MUCH FOR ME.
NOT YOU, BRITNEY. THIS IS MY FAULT.
SAMANTHA, YOU DID NOTHING WRONG. I'M SORRY. WE DETOURED THROUGH THE INNER SANCTUM TO ARM MARCUS AFTER YOUR MESSAGE AND I TOOK TOO LONG.
NO, IT'S ME. IT'S TRUE, SELA. I'M A FAILURE. I COULDN'T STOP THEM.

WHAT? WHAT WERE THEY AFTER?
BABA YAGA MEANS TO KILL TO THE DARK ONE, AND SHE DOESN'T CARE IF SHE BURNS DOWN THE WORLD IN ORDER TO DO IT.
TO BE CONTINUED!

# Grimm Fairy Tales™
# Myths & Legends

# Chapter Five:
# The Summoning, Part 3

Story by Raven Gregory, Joe Brusha, Ralph Tedesco, and Troy Brownfield

Written by Troy Brownfield and Raven Gregory • Art by Tony Donley

Colors by Marc Lewis • Letters by Jim Campbell

VENUS. BABA YAGA. THE SEA WITCH. WOMEN OF PHENOMENAL POWER.
THEY HAVE COME TO THE CRATER CALLED HELL'S DOOR IN TURKMENISTAN TO OPEN A DOORWAY OF THEIR OWN.
THEY MEAN TO CRACK OPEN A PRISON IN THE SUN ITSELF AND UNLEASH THE BEING NAMED HELIOS SO THAT THEY MAY USE HIM TO KILL MALEC, THE DARK ONE.
THEY HAVE FOUGHT FOR THE FRAGMENTS OF THE SUNSTONE NECESSARY TO ENACT THE SUMMONING. THEY HAVE LEFT MUCH DESTRUCTION IN THEIR WAKE.

FOR BABA YAGA, THIS IS THE CULMINATION OF ALL OF HER DREAMS OF REVENGE.

SHE HAS MANAGED TO PUSH ASIDE THE MURDEROUS ENMITY BETWEEN VENUS AND THE SEA WITCH, CONVINCING THEM BOTH TO WORK TOGETHER FOR A COMMON END.

IT'S ALL GOING PERFECTLY ACCORDING TO PLAN, AND BABA YAGA CAN SEE HER FONDEST WISH COMING TRUE.

BABA YAGA!
ONE PROBLEM...
PATRICIA
THE DARK ONE
HANK
GINA
MORRIGAN
CINDY
IT'S NOT THAT KIND OF FAIRY TALE.
AS A REWARD FOR THE ENDLESS AMUSEMENT THIS FARCE HAS OFFERED ME, I'LL ALLOW YOU TO KEEP YOUR HEAD IN EXCHANGE FOR THE FRAGMENTS.

SHRAAK
ERICA!
GRRRRRRRR
I'M GLAD YOU CAME! IT SAVES ME THE TROUBLE!
NO!
HSSSSS

WHAT THE HELL IS THAT?!
I DON'T KNOW! BUT IT'S NOT TOUCHING US!

NOT BAD. MIND IF I TAKE A SWING?
BE OUR GUEST.

I THINK I'LL NAME YOU RUG.

BABA'S SPELL... IT FRACTURED...

STILL WEAK... GUARDIANS OF THE NEXUS... HEAR ME.

SO MUCH THE BETTER.
NOT NOW!
OH, YES.
IT'S HER!
MARCUS JENKINS
BRITNEY WATERS
SAMANTHA DARREN
WORST. COOKOUT. EVER.
HOLY HELL.
BABA HAS MOST OF IT TOGETHER!
PIECES FIRST! GO!
SELA MATHERS

LET'S SEE HOW THIS WORKS ONE ON ONE, BABA.
SHRAAAK
BZANG

MONSTER COMING. I'M READY.
WAIT... I CAN ALMOST SENSE HIM... LIKE THE WOLVES...

I SEE THE LAST PIECE!

BABA YAGA SPOKE TRUTH AT OUR LAST MEETING! YOU SHOULD BE WITH US! I KNOW THE DARK ONE TOOK YOUR CHILD!
YOU IDIOTS ARE GOING TO DESTROY THE WHOLE PLANET DOING THIS.
DAMN IT! DON'T YOU REALIZE THAT WHAT YOU'RE DOING COULD DESTROY THE WORLD AND YOU WITH IT?
YOU HYPOCRITE! YOU WOULD RATHER L THE DARK ONE LI THAN LET US TRY?!
DID YOU HEAR HER? MALEC TOOK HER CHILD. AND THE WHOLE PLANET IS IN DANGER?
BUT... I DON'T UNDERSTAND... THAT WOMAN... PATRICIA SAID...

IF THESE FRAGMENTS CAN DESTROY THE WORLD, WHAT DOES MALEC WANT WITH IT?
HANK! HE HELPED US! HE SAVED US!

WE'RE ON THE WRONG SIDE, AREN'T WE?

YOU NEED TO MOVE. HE NEEDS OUR AID.
I DON'T THINK SO, MORRIGAN.
WHAT? YOU WOULD DEFY ME?

I GUESS I WOULD.
AND YOU KNOW THAT DEFYING ME MEANS THAT YOU DEFY YOUR MASTER?
I SUPPOSE I DO.
VERY WELL.

SHLKKK

NOOO!
GET BACK!

STOP NOW, OR THERE'S *MORE* FOR YOU.

MORRIGAN, WE NEED TO--.
HELP US! HE ATTACKED HANK!

THRUNCH
NOT NOW.
Dear God...
HANK...?
OH, HANK... NOT YOU TOO...

DAMN IT ALL, ESMERALDA! I NEED YOUR FRAGMENT!

HERE!

THERE IT IS!
SHRAAAK

FZAAAAK
ANOTHER STUPID MOVE, SAMANTHA.

AT LAST...
BABA GOT THE SUNSTONE!
I SAW! I'M--
FWAM
Samantha.
WAIT, WHAT--? OH DAMN!

SELA! THE BEAST!

GRRRRRRRR

I HAVE A GIFT, BIG FELLA. MAYBE IT'LL LET ME TALK TO YOU... CALM YOU DOWN...
WHAAP

KLANG
GO AWAY, SEA HAG! SELA IS MINE!

K-SHANNG
CUT THE CRAP, SWEETHEART. THE WORLD'S AT STAKE AND I'M THROUGH PLAYING WITH YOU.
I WOULDN'T HAVE IT ANY OTHER WAY, SPECS.

LET'S TAKE HER, SELA! SHE NEEDS TO PAY FOR SHANG!
CINDY ISN'T IMPORTANT! WE SHOULD ALL BE STOPPING BABA YAGA!

YOU DON'T HAVE TO TELL ME HOW TO DO MY JOB, SELA! I'VE BEEN FIGHTING AS THE GUARDIAN WHILE YOU CHASE WHATEVER VENDETTAS YOU HAVE!
MAYBE IF YOU'D BEEN FIGHTING AND WINNING WE WOULDN'T BE IN THIS MESS!

DO YOU EVEN *HEAR* YOURSELF, YOU SMUG *BITCH*?!

SHRAAK

THIS ISN'T *ABOUT* EVERYTHING THAT'S HAPPENED! WE NEED TO STOP BABA *NOW!*

*AW...* TOO BAD SHANG DIDN'T LIVE TO SEE *THIS.*

SHRAAAHAAAAK

NICE SHOT.
NOT BAD YOURSELF.

YEEESSS!
OH, NO...
SHE'S DONE IT...

HELIOS! COME FORTH!
HE IS GLORIOUS...
I AM... FREE?

YES, HELIOS. FREE. I, BABA YAGA, HAVE SUMMONED YOU.
WHERE IS SHE? I HAVE BEEN GONE AND SHE WAS *HERE?*
WHO?

SHE! WHERE IS *SHE?* I WANT HER.
I DON'T KNOW WHO YOU SEEK, BUT I WILL HELP YOU *FIND* HER IF YOU HELP *ME* NOW.

HE'S DISORIENTED FROM HIS *IMPRISONMENT,* BABA YAGA. ALLOW ME TO HELP.
WHAT SHOULD WE DO?

THIS.

SHRRRAKKKK

THIS JUST WENT EXTREMELY PEAR-SHAPED.
I DO NOT UNDERSTAND...
WHILE THEY'RE ALL WATCHING THE SHOW, GATHER OUR PEOPLE.
FAST.
TREACHEROUS WHORE! YOU BRING RUINATION TO EVERYTHING!
YOU DON'T KNOW THE HALF OF IT, CALAMARI.
SATISFIED?
INDEED.

THE SUNSTONE IS *MINE*. HELIOS IS *MINE*. AND THIS WORLD AND EVERYTHING ON IT NOW BELONGS TO *ME*.
TO BE CONCLUDED!

# Grimm Fairy Tales™
# Myths & Legends

# Chapter Six:
# The Summoning, Part 4

Story by Raven Gregory, Joe Brusha, Ralph Tedesco, and Troy Brownfield

Written by Troy Brownfield and Raven Gregory • Art by Josh Hood

Colors by Jason Embury • Letters by Jim Campbell

From the Chronicles of the Guardian of the Nexus, Samantha Darren...
AND NOW, TO SHOW YOU ALL THE TRUE MEANING OF POWER!
It was then, after we failed to prevent Baba Yaga from assembling the Sunstone, that all seemed LOST.
HELIOS! I BID YOU STOP.
Venus had BETRAYED Baba Yaga, and handed the Sunstone over to the Dark One.
YOU BID ME STOP?
INDEED.

It didn't go exactly as they'd PLANNED.
YEEEAAARRRGH!

BACK!
HEH. SKELETON WITH A STICK.
IMPOSSIBLE!
MORE?

DAMN YOU ALL!
WHAT'S THIS?
LEAVE HIM ALONE! HE'S MINE TO BURN!
I TOUCH YOU, YET YOU DO NOT BURN? YOU...
...ARE PUREST BEAUTY, SPIRIT AND FLAME. MY LOVE, RETURNED TO ME AFTER ALL THIS TIME?

MY LOVE, MY HEART.... WHAT WOULD YOU HAVE OF ME?
THERE'S NOTHING ELSE *LEFT* FOR ME IN THE WORLD. MY BROTHER IS DEAD. OUR FRIENDS, OUR PARENTS THERE'S *NOTHING* LEFT.
I HAVE KNOWN NOTHING BUT *IMPRISONMENT* THESE *THOUSANDS* OF YEARS, AND YOU HAVE ONLY SUFFERED. WHAT CAN I GIVE YOU?

WHAT CAN I DO TO *SOOTHE* YOUR HEART?
ONE THING.

I... ERRED. HE *CANNOT* BE CONTROLLED.
WHAT DO WE DO?
WE WITHDRAW. VENUS, YOU AND YOUR CUR COME WITH US.
ANOTHER TIME, GUARDIAN.
*WAIT!*

WELL, MY DEAR SELA, IT SEEMS THAT WE FACE A QUANDARY.
DO WE NOW?

MY PLANS ARE UNDONE. I AM BETRAYED, AND THE DARK ONE ISN'T DEAD.
I KNOW YOU'LL WANT TO BATTLE, BUT I'D JUST AS SOON TAKE THIS NEW BAUBLE AND GO.
PERHAPS YOU DIDN'T NOTICE THAT YOU SET AN INSANELY POWERFUL HIGHBORN FREE.

WHAT, DO YOU EXPECT ME TO TRY TO BOTTLE HIM? YOU TAKE ME FOR A FOOL, SAMANTHA?
OR DOES YOUR EMBARRASSMENT OVER THE HUMILIATION YOU SUFFERED AT MY HANDS EXTEND TO WANTING TO SEE ME BURN?

SHE DOESN'T EXPECT YOU TO HELP, BABA YAGA. BUT I DO.
WHAT POSSIBLE REASON--

PEOPLE ARE GOING TO DIE, BABA YAGA. MOTHERS ARE GOING TO DIE. DO YOU REMEMBER WHAT THAT'S LIKE?
DO YOU REMEMBER WHY YOU UNDERTOOK THIS QUEST?
...
THEN THE ANSWER IS EVIDENT. YOUR RECKLESS DESIRE FOR REVENGE ALLOWED YOU TO BE DUPED AND SET HELIOS FREE.
YOU TELL ME, BABA YAGA. DO YOU NEED TO MAKE THAT RIGHT?

I DO. IF FOR NO OTHER REASON THAN PREVENTING THE DARK ONE'S CERTAIN GLOATING.
ERICA AND I WILL HELP YOU. VENUS PLAYED US ALL FOR FOOLS. I WOULD ERASE THIS MESS, THEN IMPLORE YOU ALL TO CONSIDER WELL THE MENACE SHE REPRESENTS.

I WILL NOW USE MY SIGHT TO SEE WHERE HELIOS AND GINA HAVE GONE. I AM TOO WEAK TO GO WITH YOU.
I NEED TO SUMMON ANOTHER WOLF. HOW ARE YOU HOLDING UP, BIG GUY?
I WON'T LIE; THIS IS COMPLETELY INSANE. MONSTERS, MAGIC, AND THE MOST BEAUTIFUL WOMEN I'VE EVER SEEN.
EVEN THE OCTOPUS CHICK IS HOT.
EWWW.
THE TOP HALF.
AHHHH!
WHAT IS IT? DID YOU FIND THEM?
I DID. OH, I DID.
WHERE ARE THEY?
CHINA.

Later, we could only guess that Helios wanted to burn the biggest thing that Gina could conceive.
Including the trenches and natural barriers, the Ming walls stretch for more than 5,000 miles. If you count all of the branches, it's more than 13,000.

With a wave of his hand, Helios lit it all.

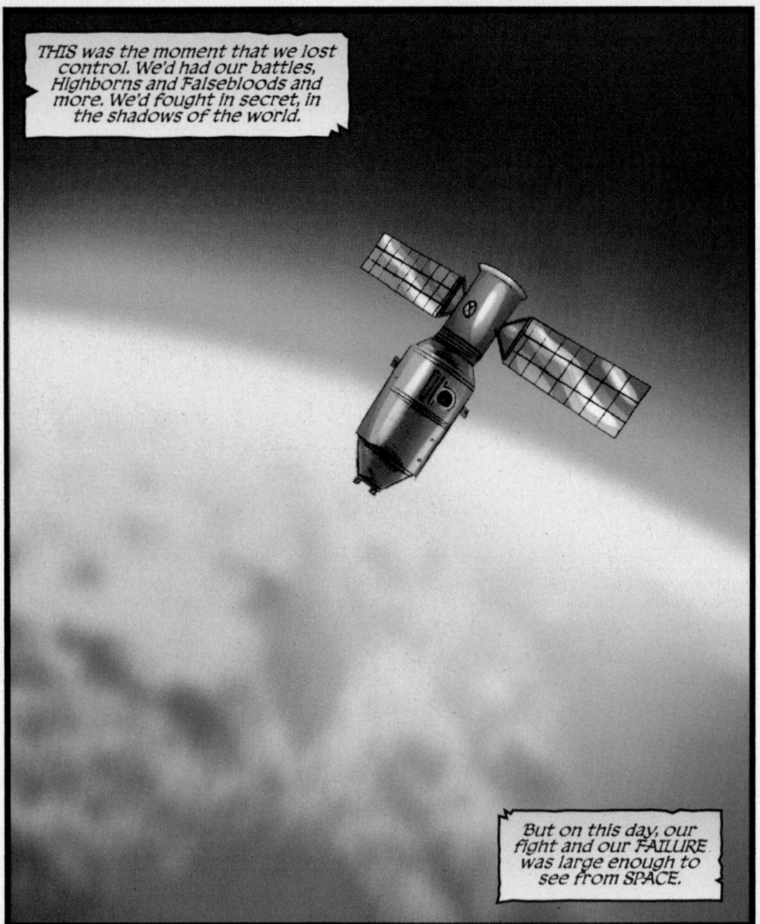
THIS was the moment that we lost control. We'd had our battles, Highborns and Falsebloods and more. We'd fought in secret, in the shadows of the world.
But on this day, our fight and our FAILURE was large enough to see from SPACE.

Aboard Tiangong-1, flight specialist Guan-yin Song looked down at her country, knowing that rivers and seas were boiling, and she wept.

She wouldn't be alone. The events put in motion by Baba Yaga would haunt us ALL.

But on that day...
HELIOS!

We fought.
KEEP HER *DOWN* WHILE I DO THE *SPELL!*
AND BE PREPARED TO HELP THE *OTHERS!*
*NO!* NOT AGAIN! IT WON'T *WORK* NOW! I ONLY GROW *MORE* POWERFUL!

I DON'T KNOW IF I CAN HOLD BACK ANOTHER SHOT LIKE THAT!
WE MUST GIVE HER TIME!
NOT AGAIN! DO YOU HEAR ME?!
AIEEEE!
GET HER!
BUT--
GO!

I LIKE YOU. YOU HAVE THE FIRE INSIDE.
WE'RE UP!
AFTER HIM!
COME THEN! COME AND BURN!
NOW I'LL--
HEAR ME, HELIOS!
NO! NOT THAT!

IT MAY NOT WORK ON *YOU,* BUT IT *WILL* WORK ON *HER.*
*SUBMIT,* HELIOS. OR GINA TAKES *YOUR* PLACE IN THE PRISON IN THE *SUN.*

NOT MY LOVE! NOT *THAT* FATE!
THEN SUBMIT, HELIOS. SUBMIT TO *ME.*

YOU DEMENTED BITCH. YOU *CAN'T* CONTROL HIM.
I CAN. AND I *WILL.*
*KNEEL,* HELIOS.

I AM YOUR SERVANT.

EXCELLENT. FIRST, YOU SHALL DIMINISH THE FLAMES. THEN...

OH, MY GOD!

IT'S *BROKEN!*

IF *I* CANNOT POSSESS HIS POWER, *NO ONE* WILL! THE STONE IS *SHATTERED!*

*KILL THEM ALL!*

HELIOS!
HE MEANS TO KILL GINA!
YOU... WILL... BE... ASHES!

NO! MORRIGAN! AWAY!
HE RAN AGAIN.

THE BASTARD LEFT US!

NOW IS THE TIME! SOMEONE KILL VENUS!

ENOUGH OF YOU!

ENOUGH OF YOU.

SELA, LET'S NOT REPEAT OUR MISTAKE. CALM.

YOU'RE RIGHT. HELIOS, WE WANT EVERYONE TO CALM DOWN SO THAT WE CAN SPEAK WITH YOU. JUST SPEAK.

YOU WOULD... SPEAK?
YES. I DON'T WANT TO HURT YOU OR GINA. I DON'T WANT ANYONE HURT. WE JUST WANT TO STOP THE WORLD FROM BURNING.

DON'T LISTEN TO HER! SHE MEANS TO KILL GINA AND IMPRISON YOU AGAIN!
NONE OF YOU CAN BE TRUSTED!
AAAAAARRRGGGH!
FWSSSSHHH

THEY'RE GONE! HELIOS AND GINA!
DON'T GET ANY IDEAS. YOU'RE IN THIS UNTIL THEY'RE CONTAINED.
MY FACE! DAMN YOU ALL!
SELA! KILL HER NOW!
HOLD ME.
A CURSE ON TELEPORTATION! WILL THIS WOMAN'S LIFE NEVER END?!
PERHAPS NOT, ESMERALDA. AS MUCH AS WE'D LIKE IT, THIS WASN'T VENUS' DAY. OR THE DARK ONE'S.
WHAT NOW?

HEAR ME NOW!
I CAN'T MAINTAIN THIS COMMUNICATION FOR LONG!
WE'RE LISTENING.
THE MEANS TO BANISH HELIOS IS LOST, BUT THE KEY GEM IS INTACT. THERE'S ONE HOPE LEFT. DEPOWERING.
SHE'S RIGHT!
THERE WAS A WORKING ON THE MAP I TOOK FROM THE INNER SANCTUM. THEY'LL STILL BE POWERFUL, BUT HE WON'T BE GODLIKE.
WE COULD DEFEAT THEM.
WE'LL HAVE TO DO A HELL OF A LOT BETTER THAN WE HAVE BEEN. WE NEED A REAL PLAN.
I CAN DO THE WORKING, BUT SOMEONE HAS TO GET CLOSE TO HELIOS WITH THE GEM.

I'LL DO IT. SO MUCH OF THIS IS *MY* FAULT.

SAMANTHA...

BUT IT *IS.* IF YOU CAN HOLD HIM OFF, I CAN HOLD *THIS.*

*HURRY.* THEY ARE NEAR. HE ONLY MOVED THEM A FEW MILES DOWN THE WALL. HIS GRIP ON HIS SANITY *LOOSENS.*

YOU LADIES MENTIONED A *PLAN?* IT SO HAPPENS THAT I *HAVE* ONE.

TEN MILES AWAY--
MY LOVE, ARE YOU WELL?
I'LL BE OKAY. BABA YAGA HIT ME HARDER THAN I THOUGHT.
DAMN THEM ALL! I'LL BURN THEM UNTIL THEIR MELTING EYES FLOW DOWN THEIR CHEEKS LIKE MOLTEN LAVA.
HELIOS... I...
YES, MY LOVE?
I DON'T WANT THEM TO CHASE US. I JUST WANT US TO ESCAPE.
THEY WILL CONTINUE TO PURSUE US. WE MUST MEET THEM AND MAKE THEM BURN.

WHAT DEVILRY?
THEY'RE *HERE!*
*COWARDS!* COWARDS IN A SEA OF DARKNESS!
HELIOS...
YES, LOVE?

GOTCHA.
WHA--
STAY WHERE YOU ARE, HELIOS!
I WILL *NOT* GO BACK THERE!
WE KNOW.

As I stood there in disbelief that it was working and that I wasn't being burned alive, it occurred to me that shifting that much magic and energy at once might have a CONSEQUENCE.
I'd be proven right on another day. But in that moment, finally...

Our plan had WORKED. And I hadn't failed.
ARE YOU OKAY?
LISTEN TO ME, QUICKLY NOW.
YOU STILL RETAIN A MEASURE OF YOUR POWER, BUT YOU ARE NO MATCH FOR THEM. COME WITH ME, AND WE'LL KILL THE DARK ONE TOGETHER.
FOR HANK?
FOR HANK. AND MY MOTHER.
DAMN IT!
THE SEA WITCH AND ERICA ARE GONE, TOO.
I'LL MISS THEM.
HAHAHAHA!
I'M PRETTY SURE I JUST MISSED SOMETHING.

YOU DIDN'T MISS A THING. GREAT PLAN, MARCUS.
THANKS; I HOPE I DID MY PART.

WHAT DO WE DO NOW?
SLEEP FOR A WEEK?

I'M SERIOUS; DO WE GO AFTER BABA YAGA? I'M NOT A FAN OF THE SEA WITCH, BUT SHOULD WE HUNT DOWN VENUS?
THAT'S... COMPLICATED.

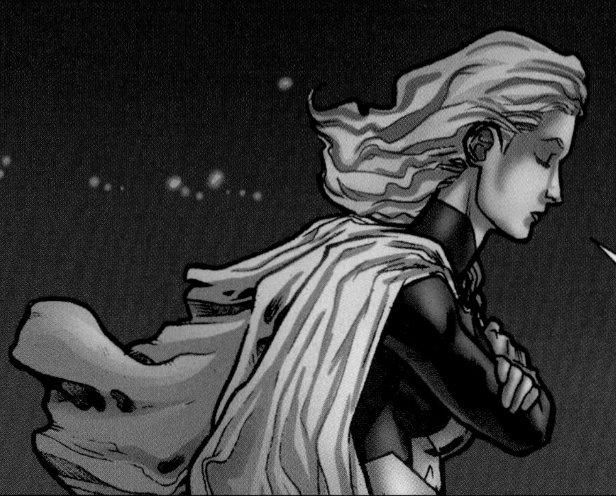
SPEAKING OF THE SEA WITCH, I'D LIKE TO TRY AND GET ERICA AWAY FROM HER AGAIN. AND THERE'S THE MATTER OF THE DARK ONE.

SOMETHING NEEDS TO BE DONE.
YOU'RE THE GUARDIAN. YOU TELL ME.
BURDEN OF THE GUARDIAN. BUT OUR FRIENDS HAVE ALWAYS BEEN WILLING TO SHARE THAT BURDEN.
MORE UARDIANS?
MORE LIKE A GROUP. VOLUNTEERS. US, MAYBE SOMEONE LIKE CROSS...
SOUNDS LIKE YOU WANT SOLDIERS.
YOU'VE BEEN A SOLDIER. WHAT IF I TOLD YOU IT WAS TIME TO BE A KNIGHT?

HIDE YOURSELF. I MUST DECIDE WHAT TO DO ABOUT ILYS.
MOTHER? I'M HERE.
WHAT'S WRONG?
I'M... UNWELL.
STAY OUTSIDE.
IS THERE ANYTHING I CAN DO?
NO, CHILD.

PLEASE GO BACK TO BED. I'LL SEE YOU SOON.
MY FACE. MY BEAUTIFUL, PERFECT FACE.
DAMN YOU, SELA.
DAMN YOU!
SKAASH

EPILOGUE I:

IS THERE ANYTHING WE CAN DO?

THANK YOU, CINDY, BUT NO. I WISH TO BE ALONE.
WE SHALL BE NEAR IF YOU REQUIRE IT.
MASTER, MAY I--

YES, PATRICIA, BY ALL MEANS. NOTIFY MORRIGAN WHEN YOU'VE RETURNED. NOW *LEAVE* ME.

HERE TO *GLOAT,* CHILD-THING?

NO. I JUST WANT YOU TO RECOGNIZE SOMETHING. I WANT YOU TO KNOW AND UNDERSTAND. I HAVE SEEN WHAT IS TO COME.
AND THAT IS?
YOU KNOW THAT BABA YAGA WILL KILL YOU. YOU KNOW THIS IS COMING.
BARRING THAT ALMOST INEVITABLE CERTAINTY, YOU WILL FINALLY PUSH SELA TOO FAR AND YOU WILL END YOUR EXISTENCE TWITCHING ON THE END OF HER SWORD. THESE THINGS ARE TRUE.

WHY ARE YOU TELLING ME THIS? YOU, OF ALL PEOPLE?
BECAUSE I WANT YOU TO TAKE COMFORT.
TAKE COMFORT?

YES. TAKE COMFORT IN THE FACT THAT YOU'RE JUST GOING TO DIE.
WHAT AWAITS EVERYONE ELSE IS GOING TO BE SO MUCH WORSE.

EPILOGUE II:

--TODAY'S SPECIAL SESSION APPROVED AID AND MEASURES STEMMING FROM THE RECENT--
KLIK

--INCIDENT IN CHINA, AS WELL AS OTHER RECORDED INSTANCES IN NEW YORK AND TURKEY--
KLIK

--CAN'T DENY THE EVIDENCE OF OUR OWN EYES. THESE PEOPLE OF INCREDIBLE POWER ARE REAL, AND--
KLIK

--IT'S ALL A SIGN, A SIGN THAT THE END TIMES HAVE COME! IT'S WRITTEN!
BRRING
BRRING

THE FIRST ANGEL BLEW HIS TRUMPET, AND THERE FOLLOWED HAIL AND FIRE, MIXED WITH BLOOD, AND THESE WERE THROWN UPON THE EARTH! WE HAVE SEEN THESE THINGS!
KLIK
WE'RE A GO?

SCRAMBLE THE TEAM. WHEELS UP IN TWENTY.

CAROLYN "CARRIE" BRADDOCK
HI, BABY. I'M SORRY THAT I COULDN'T MAKE SELA PAY FOR YOU, YET. BUT MOMMY PROMISES.

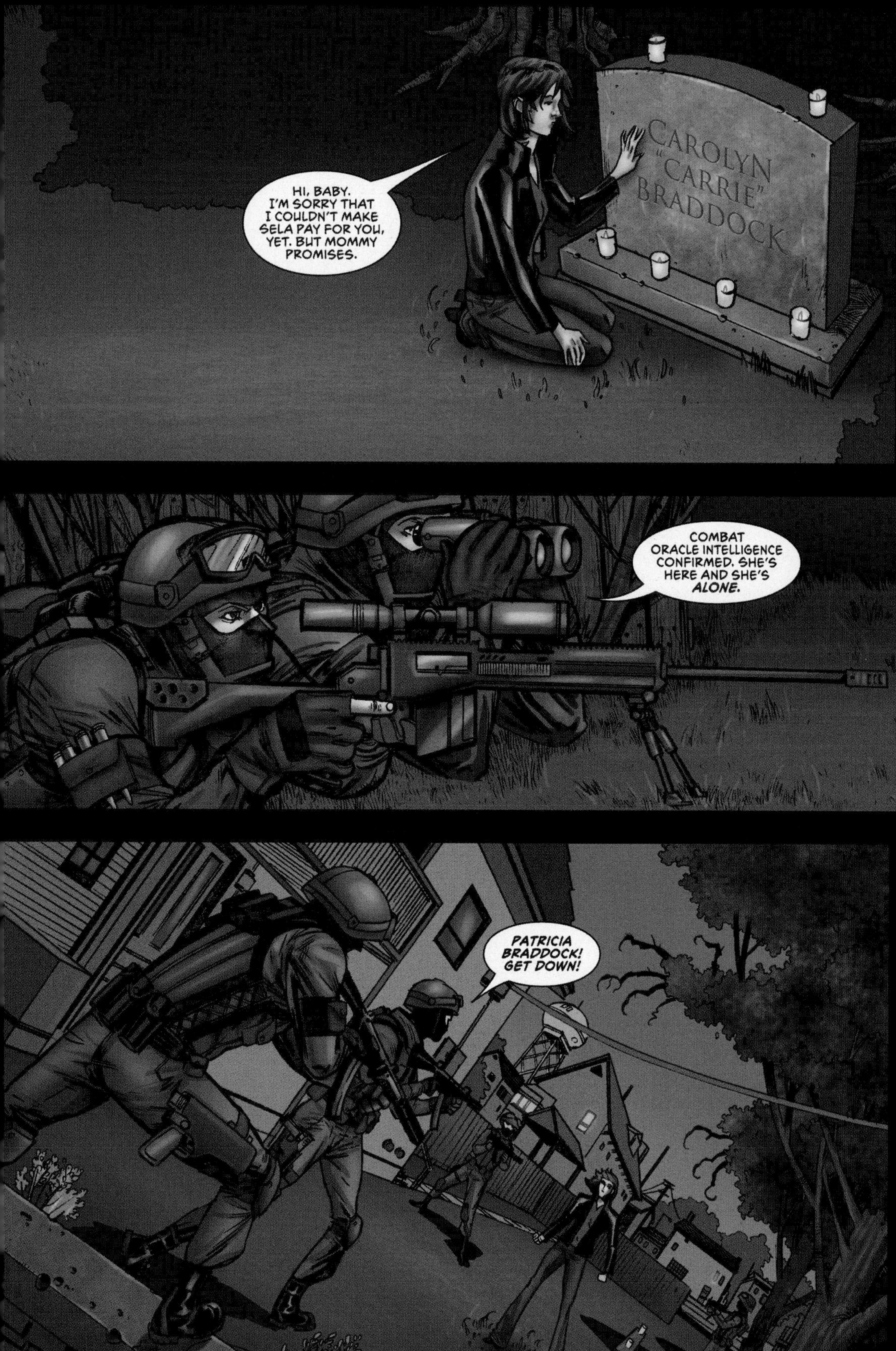

COMBAT ORACLE INTELLIGENCE CONFIRMED. SHE'S HERE AND SHE'S *ALONE.*

*PATRICIA BRADDOCK! GET DOWN!*

BRRRAKK
LEAVE ME ALONE!

STAND DOWN!

I SAID--
LEAVE ME ALONE!

I WARNED YOU!
SHRKKT

ONE IS DOWN!
TAKE HER OUT!

KRAKK

WIERZBOWSKI IS KIA, NO OTHER SIGNIFICANT INJURIES. CONFIRMED KILL ON THE HOSTILE, SIR. WE'LL BAG ONE ALIVE NEXT TIME. HOPEFULLY, THEY'RE ALL THIS EASY TO KILL.

EPILOGUE III:

MYST. THE GUARDIAN GRAVEYARD--

AH, SHANG. YOUR PROTÉGÉS ARE ABOUT TO FACE THEIR MOST **SEVERE** TEST. THE **INNOCENT** THOUGHT THAT I SHOULD HELP, EVEN THOUGH INTERFERENCE HAS NEVER BEEN IN MY **NATURE.**

AND YET, I HAVE SEEN THE ROAD FOR SELA, SAMANTHA, AND THOSE THEY WOULD CALL THEIR KNIGHTS.

THEY WILL NEED VICTORIES TO BALANCE THE COMING HORRORS AND LOSS.

THEY WILL NEED YOU.
~THE END~
Thank you for reading GRIMM FAIR TALES MYTHS & LEGENDS! Follo Sela and Samantha as the battle f the fate of the GRIMM UNIVERSE continues!

# Grimm Fairy Tales™
# Myths & Legends

# Cover Gallery

Grimm Fairy Tales Myths & Legends #16 Cover A
Artwork by Stjepan Sejic

Grimm Fairy Tales Myths & Legends #16 Cover B
Artwork by Robert Atkins • Colors by Sanju Nivangune

Grimm Fairy Tales Myths & Legends #16 Boston Comic Con Exclusive Cover
Artwork by Elias Chatzoudis

Grimm Fairy Tales Myths & Legends #17 Cover A
Artwork by Ale Garza • Colors by Sanju Nivangune

Grimm Fairy Tales Myths & Legends #17 Cover B

Grimm Fairy Tales Myths & Legends #17 Phoenix Comic Con Exclusive Cover
Artwork by Eric Basaldua • Colors by Nei Ruffino

Grimm Fairy Tales Myths & Legends #17 Phoenix Comic Con Exclusive Cover
Artwork by Eric Basaldua • Colors by Nei Ruffino

Grimm Fairy Tales Myths & Legends #22 Connecting Covers A & B
Artwork by Giuseppe Gafaro • Colors by Ula Mos

Grimm Fairy Tales Myths & Legends #22 Wizard World Austin Exclusive Cover
Artwork by Elias Chatzoudis

Grimm Fairy Tales Myths & Legends #23 Cover A
Artwork by Giuseppe Cafaro • Colors by Romulo Fajardo Jr.

Grimm Fairy Tales Myths & Legends #23 Cover B
Artwork by Eric J • Colors by Linda Luksic Sejic

Grimm Fairy Tales Myths & Legends #24 Cover A
Artwork by Alfredo Reyes • Colors by Linda Luksoc-Sejic

Grimm Fairy Tales Myths & Legends #24 Cover B
Artwork by Anthony Spay • Colors by Ivan Nunes

Grimm Fairy Tales Myths & Legends #25 Cover A
Artwork by Alfredo Reyes • Colors by Stephen Schaffer

Grimm Fairy Tales Myths & Legends #25 Cover B
Artwork by Mike Lilly • Colors by Jason Embury

A SHADOW FALLS OVER THE GRIMM UNIVERSE...
Grimm Fairy Tales
presents:
UNLEASHED
THE BIGGEST GRIMM UNIVERSE EVENT BEGINS APRIL 2013!
FOR MORE INFORMATION ON UNLEASHED VISIT BLOG.ZENESCOPE.COM AND FACEBOOK.COM/ZENESCOPE

# DON'T MISS ANY OF THE ACTION!

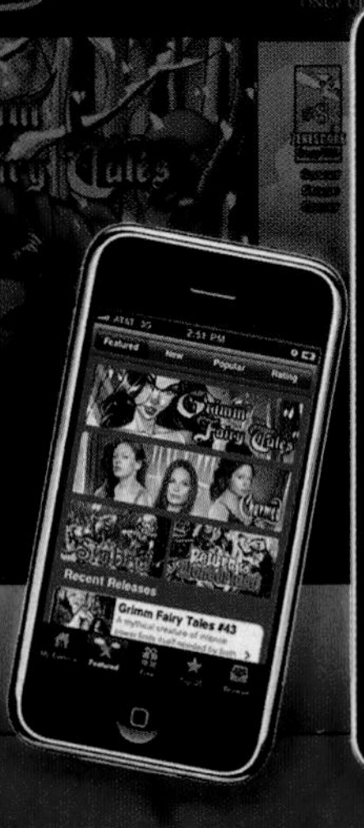

DOWNLOAD THE OFFICIAL ZENESCOPE DIGITAL COMICS APP FROM ITUNES TODAY!

APPLICATION REQUIRES APPLE IPHONE, IPAD OR ITOUCH

POWERED BY COMIXOLOGY

ARE YOU READY TO P[illegible]AY?

MEGATOUCH AND ZENESCOPE ENTERTAINMENT PRESENTS

# Grimm Fairy Tales Photo Hunt

SOLVE ALL 30 ROUNDS OF PLAY!

only $4.99

Available on the App Store

OVER 1,000 IMAGES FROM THE GRIMM UNIVERSE!

DOWNLOAD IT TODAY!

Megatouch

2012 MEGATOUCH ALL RIGHTS RESERVED.
2012 ZENESCOPE ENTERTAINMENT, INC. ALL RIGHTS RESERVED.

# BRING THE UNIVERSE TO LIFE WITH ZENESCOPE AR!

SCHNEPP · BRUSHA · TEDESCO
Grimm Fairy Tales
ANIMATED ONE-SHOT
zenescope
$3.99 U.S.
Cover A

Grimm Fairy Tales
GIANT-SIZE

zenescope
$7.99 U.S. COVER A
a/corona
CÆSARTIST
AR ENABLED

**UNLOCK EPIC TRAILERS, BONUS COMMENTARY, AND INTERACTIVE CONTENT RIGHT FROM THE PALM OF YOUR HAND!**

**IT'S EASY! JUST DOWNLOAD ZENESCOPE AR FROM THE APPLE APPSTORE OR GOOGLE PLAY AND SCAN ANY ZENESCOPE AR BRANDED COVER TO GET EXCLUSIVE CONTENT.**

ZENESCOPE AR

POWERED

©2012 ZENESCOPE ENTERTAINMENT, INC. ALL RIGHTS RESERVED.

WWW.ZENESCOPE.COM • FACEBOOK.COM/ZENESCOPE

ZENESCOPE ENTERTAINMENT PRESENTS

# Wonderland
## The Board Game

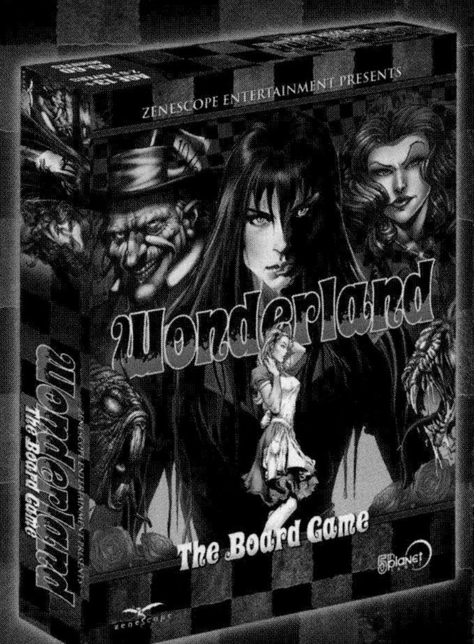


## ON SALE NOW!

Experience the madness that is Wonderland!

Calie, her friends and her enemies fall between the real world that is ripe with danger and an even deadlier realm that exists on the other side of the Looking Glass. Win epic battles against Cheshire, Jabberwocky, and a host of other deadly foes, all the while keeping from the brink of insanity...or diving right over its edge. Based on one of the top comic book series from Zenescope Entertainment, experience Wonderland in a way no one has ever experienced before... a vibrant, twisted world full of surprises, right in your living room!

WONDERLAND BOARD GAME
2-6 Players
Packaging: Approx. 12" x 8.75" x 1.75"
SRP: $39.99

VISIT ZENESCOPE.COM FOR MORE INFORMATION!

Grimm Fairy Tales™
Myths & Legends